MODERN WORLD NATIONS

MODERN WORLD NATIONS

Germany

Second Edition

William R. Horne
University of Northern British Columbia
with additional text by Zoran Pavlović

Series Editor
Charles F. Gritzner
South Dakota State University

CHELSEA HOUSE
PUBLISHERS
An imprint of Infobase Publishing

Frontispiece: Flag of Germany

Cover: Colorful houses line the banks of the Kocher River in Schwäbisch Hall, in the southern German state of Baden-Württemberg.

Germany, Second Edition

Copyright © 2007 by Infobase Publishing

All rights reserved. No part of this book may be reproduced or utilized in any form or by any means, electronic or mechanical, including photocopying, recording, or by any information storage or retrieval systems, without permission in writing from the publisher. For information contact:

Chelsea House
An imprint of Infobase Publishing
132 West 31st Street
New York NY 10001

Library of Congress Cataloging-in-Publication Data
Horne, William Reginald.
  Germany / William R. Horne ; with additional text by Zoran Pavlovic.—2nd ed.
    p. cm. — (Modern world nations)
  Includes bibliographical references and index.
  ISBN-13: 978-0-7910-9512-6 (hardcover)
  ISBN-10: 0-7910-9512-6 (hardcover)
  1. Germany—Juvenile literature.   2. Germany—Social life and customs—Juvenile literature.   3. Germany—Civilization—Juvenile literature.   I. Pavlovic, Zoran.   II. Title.   III. Series.

DD17.H67 2007
943—dc22   2007010456

Chelsea House books are available at special discounts when purchased in bulk quantities for businesses, associations, institutions, or sales promotions. Please call our Special Sales Department in New York at (212) 967-8800 or (800) 322-8755.

You can find Chelsea House on the World Wide Web at http://www.chelseahouse.com

Series design by Takeshi Takahashi

Cover design by Joo Young An

Printed in the United States of America

Bang NMSG 10 9 8 7 6 5 4 3 2 1

This book is printed on acid-free paper.

All links and Web addresses were checked and verified to be correct at the time of publication. Because of the dynamic nature of the Web, some addresses and links may have changed since publication and may no longer be valid.

Table of Contents

Germany

Second Edition

1

Introducing Germany

A review of twentieth-century history would be incomplete without reference to Germany. During the past century, Germany was involved in two world wars. Following its defeat in World War II, its division into East and West became a major symbol of the larger division of the postwar world, just as its reunification in 1990 served as a symbol of the cold war's end. Today, as the major power in the European Union, it is poised to be a leader in the twenty-first century. The United States, too, has powerful historical ties to Germany. Germans represent the nation's largest single ethnic group and many traits of American culture can be traced to German roots. The Protestant Reformation, for example, began in Germany, and many other "American" characteristics—from words in our vocabulary (angst, kindergarten, sauerkraut), to what and how we eat, to the idea that sparked the Interstate Highway System—have German origins.

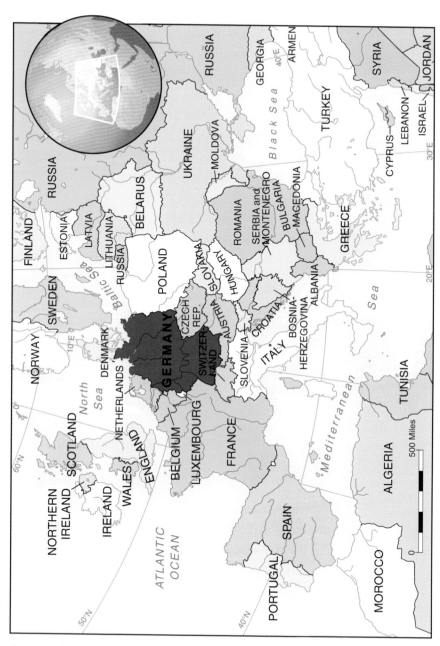

Germany is located in central Europe and shares borders with nine countries: Austria, Belgium, the Czech Republic, Denmark, France, Luxembourg, the Netherlands, Poland, and Switzerland. Germany is slightly smaller than the state of Montana and is Europe's sixth-largest country (in terms of area).

Germany's population is the largest in Europe (excluding Russia) and its economy is the continent's most powerful. Roughly one of every seven Europeans is German. Economically, the country is Europe's leader in industry, trade, and services. The country was one of the first on mainland Europe to actively participate in the Industrial Revolution, after its spread from the United Kingdom in the early nineteenth century. Two centuries later, it also played a key role in the formation of the European Union (EU).

Germany is located in the heart of Europe. To the west it borders the Netherlands, Belgium, Luxembourg, and France. To the south lie Switzerland, Austria, and the Czech Republic, to the east is Poland, and to the north Denmark. The North European Plain, which includes the densely populated northern third of Germany, has been a route for human migration and a battlefield for roving armies since ancient times.

European countries are often thought of as being very old, but modern Germany is younger than the United States. The German Empire was created in 1871 as a union of more than 30 smaller states. Because each state had its own capital, Germany today has many large cities scattered throughout the country; although the current capital city, Berlin, is the country's largest urban center.

Twice during the twentieth century, Germany tried to expand outward from its central location to take control of its neighbors by force. World War I (1914–1918) and World War II (1939–1945) were the greatest conflicts of the century. On both occasions, the late entry of the United States into these wars in 1917 and 1941 tipped the scales against Germany. Unable to fight a war on two fronts, Germany was pushed back, losing some of its original territory in both wars.

After World War II, in addition to losing territory, the remainder of the country was occupied by foreign troops and divided into occupation zones that eventually formed two separate countries, East Germany and West Germany. East

Germany was the satellite state of the Soviet Union and one of the strongest economic powers in the East European Socialist block. West Germany joined the countries of Western Europe and became an even stronger economic power.

When North American and Western European countries organized the North Atlantic Treaty Organization (NATO) in 1949 to protect democracy, the Soviet Union countered in 1955 by unifying the countries of Eastern Europe into the Warsaw Pact. The two forces faced each other along the border between West and East Germany. This border became known as the *Iron Curtain.* This term, which became synonymous with the cold war in Europe, was first used in a 1946 speech delivered by British statesman Sir Winston Churchill in Fulton, Missouri.

The dream of German reunification grew dimmer and dimmer as the years passed. Then, quite suddenly, in 1990, East and West Germany were reunited. The removal of that border was instrumental in the breakup of the Warsaw Pact and the creation of a new dynamic in Europe. NATO added three other former Warsaw Pact members: Poland, Hungary, and the Czech Republic.

German reunification was seen as a major challenge, because there were great social, political, and economic differences between the East and West. Since unification, however, there has been a significant transformation in the East. It has become increasingly integrated with the West both economically and socially. The cost of reunification, however, has been high for the former West Germany in terms of the financial strain on the country. Under Soviet control, East Germany's economy lagged far behind that of the West.

Today the European Union has a population approximately equal to that of the United States, and it has become a global economic power with Germany as its strongest member. Some countries are concerned that Germany has the power to take over economically what it could not take by force. As of 2007, Germany is the world's largest exporter of goods (although

On November 9, 1989, the East German government opened its border with West Germany, and the Berlin Wall, long a symbol of the cold war, was toppled. Pictured here in front of the Brandenburg Gate are East and West German citizens celebrating the fall of the Berlin Wall, which served as the border between West Berlin and East Germany for 28 years.

China will likely surpass it in the next couple of years). In addition, it is an active member of the Group of Seven (G7) (and the Group of Eight, which includes Russia as the eighth member). German industry is well known for its high quality precision instruments and automobiles such as Volkswagen, Audi, Mercedes, and BMW.

The current geography of any area is the result of the interaction of many forces. This book begins with an outline of physical environmental conditions in the Federal Republic of Germany, as the reunited Germany is called today. Although modern Germany is a relatively new country, the area has been inhabited for a very long time. Chapter 3 introduces the political and social changes that shaped the unique history of the country. Chapter 4 presents the demographic characteristics of the current population and its relationship to the past.

Government policies have a significant influence on how natural resources are used and the economy develops. Chapter 5 discusses the government of modern Germany and its development since 1871. Chapters 6 and 7 are about the economy and how it relates to the living conditions of the people. Future prospects for Germany are considered in the final chapter. The interaction of demographic, political, cultural, social, technological, and economic change has formed the modern landscape of Germany and provides the basis for future developments. Look for these relationships throughout this book.

2

Physical
Landscapes

Germany has an area of 137,847 square miles (357,021 square kilometers). It stretches about 520 miles (840 kilometers) north to south, reaching from 47 to 55 degrees north latitude, and 385 miles (620 kilometers) east to west, between 6 and 15 degrees east longitude. The terrain can be divided into three regions that increase in elevation from north to south. Each is unique in terms of natural resources and human activities.

Germany has 1,485 miles (2,389 kilometers) of coastline facing the North Sea to the west and Baltic Sea to the east. A break in the coast is created by the Jutland Peninsula, which predominantly belongs to Denmark (although the southern half of the peninsula is occupied by the German state of Schleswig-Holstein). The two seas are connected south of the peninsula by the Kiel Canal. Germany has a 12-mile territorial water limit and a 200-mile exclusive economic zone, which represent a mutually agreed upon international standard. Because of the shape of the coastline and the proximity to other countries, however, the actual area claimed is quite small.

The coastline is generally low lying with sandy beaches and marshlands. In the summer, the beaches of both the North and Baltic seas are popular holiday destinations. Shrimp and mussels abound in the mudflats and tidal waters along parts of the coast.

In some areas, marshes have been reclaimed, similar to the *polder* lands of the Netherlands. These areas provide rich pastureland and a landscape of dairy farms and fields of vegetables. Other low coastal areas contain peat bogs. Peat is primarily made up of moss, which can be spread on lawns and gardens to improve growth, or dried and burned as a fuel. Where peat has been removed, a landscape of shallow ponds is created.

THE NORTH GERMAN PLAIN

South of the Baltic and North sea coastlines is the low, gently rolling North German Plain. This almost featureless landscape is part of the huge North European Plain, which extends westward to the Pyrenees Mountains, through the Netherlands, Belgium, and France, and eastward through Poland, Belarus, and Russia to the Ural Mountains.

Five northward-flowing rivers cross the plain. From west to east, they are the Rhine, Ems, Weser, Elbe, and Oder. The Rhine is the largest of these rivers. Beginning in Switzerland, it flows through Germany and into the Netherlands, reaching the North Sea at Rotterdam, the world's busiest seaport. The Ems, a shorter river, reaches the North Sea at Emden. Germany's largest fishing port, Bremerhaven, is located at the mouth of the Weser. The larger city of Bremen is farther downstream. The city of Hamburg, with a population of 2 million, is a port near the mouth of the Elbe River. The Oder forms the boundary between Germany and Poland and empties into the Baltic Sea. The mouth of the river is in Poland.

Regions near the Atlantic Ocean and the North Sea experience a maritime climate. Winds blowing from the west, having

Germany stretches about 520 miles (840 kilometers) north to south and 385 miles (620 kilometers) east to west. Germany can be divided into three geographical regions: the lowlands in the north, the uplands in the center, and the Bavarian Alps in the south.

passed over warm water, have a moderating effect. Summers average 61°F (16°C) and winter snow lasts for only short periods. Unpleasant weather can occur when winter storms move in from the east, often causing freezing rain. This happens when cold air masses from Siberia expand southward during wintertime and clash with moist Atlantic air over Germany. Moving away from the North Sea to the south and east, the climate becomes less maritime and more continental, with warmer summers and colder winters. The Rhine River usually remains largely ice-free, but the Elbe River often freezes in winter. Most of the lowland area receives between 20 and 30 inches (50 and 75 centimeters) of precipitation per year.

Continental glaciation, the advance of huge ice masses during the ice age, has left deposits of clay, gravel, and sand across the plain, which accounts for the soil's limited fertility. The natural vegetation across the North German Plain would be deciduous forest; however, most of this woodland has been removed to clear land for farming during the past 1,000 years. Going back into time, large areas of Europe were covered by dense forest. One could enter the forest in Portugal and walk through dense stands of trees all the way to Germany and on into Russia without ever leaving it, but that is no longer possible. Nowadays, here, as throughout the remainder of Germany, most woodlands are in areas that are protected or marked by rugged terrain. The modern landscape is one of pasturelands and grain crops. Barley is grown along the Baltic Coast, oats near the North Sea, and rye farther inland. Potatoes are another traditional crop. However, due to modern agricultural methods, the widespread use of chemical fertilizers, and improved hybrid strains that mature during a shorter growing season, many farmers have changed to corn, which is a more valuable crop.

Grains are grown to feed animals, and herds of sheep or cattle have traditionally grazed among the fields of this landscape. Livestock herding can only be done, however, where the quality of the soil provides sufficient grass and grains upon which the stock can feed. Today, most chickens, pigs, and cattle are raised in large barns and provided with grain to eat. They do not go outside to graze. This means that there is no longer a close link between agriculture and soil quality, and farm animals are less often seen when traveling in the countryside.

When the glaciers retreated around 10,000 years ago, they left gravel ridges, called moraines, which spread east to west across the plain. Examination of the main rivers on a map reveals that although they generally run south to north, most turn sharply to either the east or west as they pass through the valleys between the moraines. Today, these portions of the rivers are connected by the Mittelland Canal, which runs east to west across the North German Plain. The cities of Essen, Hanover, and Berlin are on the canal. The sedimentary rock beneath the North German Plain holds some natural gas and oil deposits. These are found north of the Mittelland Canal and contribute to Germany's petrochemical industry.

Along the southern margin of the plain, *loess* (windblown silt) deposits create extremely fertile soils that support sugar beets, wheat, and corn. About a third of Germany's land is suitable for raising crops and another 15 percent is meadow or pastureland. The cities of Cologne, Düsseldorf, Essen, Hanover, Leipzig, and Dresden dot the southern edge of the North German Plain. These cities provide access to both the best agricultural land of the plain and the forest and mineral resources of the uplands to the south. All of these cities have populations between 500,000 and one million people, making the landscape different from either France or Poland, where only one city—Paris and Warsaw, respectively—dominates the urban structure. Fruits, vegetables, and flowers are grown close to these urban markets.

Beneath the southern edge of the North German Plain, a broad east-west band of coal crosses the country. In the west, it is the black, high-quality bituminous variety that can be used to produce coke for the production of steel. The industrial city of Essen, on the Ruhr River, developed on this coalfield.

In the east, the coal is the lower grade known as brown lignite. Lignite is not suitable for steel production but can be used to provide energy for factories and electricity generation. Potash is the other main mineral found on the North German Plain, particularly near the city of Hanover.

The largest city on the North German Plain has no relationship to the physical features or natural resources of the area. Berlin is the seventh-largest city in Europe. It is an artificial product of the central governments of Prussia and Germany. The city was established as the capital because of its central location at a time when Germany extended farther east than it does today.

THE CENTRAL UPLANDS

South of the North German Plain, the land becomes increasingly rugged due to the geological process of faulting. This creates steep-sided, flat-topped hills that because of erosion have become rounded in appearance. The highest elevations in this zone are found in the Black Forest, in the southwest corner of Germany, just east of the Upper Rhine, where the hills rise to 4,898 feet (1,493 meters). The Bohemian Forest and Ore Mountains on the border with the Czech Republic reach 2,536 feet (773 meters), and the Harz Mountains, which form the boundary with the North German Plain, to the southeast of Hanover, reach 3,747 feet (1,142 meters).

The Rhine, Weser, and Elbe rivers flow through the valleys between these hills, sometimes in steep-sided gorges. South of Bonn, the Rhine Gorge is a popular tourist attraction. The Rhine Valley in the southwest is the warmest part of Germany. The mean summer temperature is 66°F (19°C) and the average January temperature is just above freezing. The Black Forest to the east and the Vosges Mountains in France, to the west, create a sheltered environment. The valley sides are used for vineyards. Early Christian monks from Italy introduced grapes into the Rhine Valley for the production of wine. Vineyards are also

Originating in the Alps of Switzerland, the Rhine is Germany's longest river. More than two-thirds of the 865-mile- (1,392-kilometer-) long Rhine flows through Germany, and the river is one of Europe's primary transport routes for economic goods.

found along the Moselle, Saar, Main, and Neckar rivers. The valley floors have rich alluvial soils. Wheat, corn, sugar beets, tobacco, hops, fruits, and specialty vegetables such as asparagus are grown here.

The Central Uplands are not high enough to be a climate barrier; however, rainfall increases with elevation—reaching up to 59 inches (150 centimeters)—and temperatures decline.

There is abundant snowfall in the winter, continuing well into March. By 1800, the rivers provided waterpower for industry and today the Central Uplands provide water for the cities of the North German Plain.

Much of the Central Uplands region is forested. River valleys have alder, willow, and poplar where it is wet, and oak, ash, and elm in drier locations. Maple, chestnut, and walnut trees are also found in some areas. In the nineteenth century, the forests were cut to provide charcoal for the smelting of local iron ores into metal goods. The discovery of coal as a power source moved this industry to the nearby Ruhr Valley (Essen) in the west, and Chemnitz and Dresden in the east. Many areas have now been reforested. The Black Forest and the Jura Mountains are popular tourist destinations, and there are numerous national and state parks, where Germans can enjoy their favorite pastime of hiking. The Central Uplands also have small deposits of zinc, lead, silver, copper, and uranium. Most of the mines have closed because they are no longer profitable.

Farther south, the land is a series of plateaus crossed by the Main and Neckar rivers, both of which flow into the Rhine. The main city on the Neckar River is Stuttgart, while Frankfurt is on the Main River and Nuremberg (Nürnberg) is on the Rhine-Main-Danube Canal. The Danube River forms the southern boundary of this area. It flows eastward from the Black Forest across southern Germany and into Austria, eventually reaching the Black Sea. A canal has been built to connect the Danube to the Main.

THE ALPINE REGION

The Bavarian, or German, Alps occupy the extreme southern part of Germany. These mountains are a northern extension of the Alpine system that extends across portions of Austria and Switzerland, as well as into northern Italy and eastern France. The Alps are high, folded mountains similar to the Rocky Mountains of the United States. Their spectacular terrain is the

Rising to an elevation of 9,721 feet (2,963 meters), Zugspitze is Germany's highest point. Located in southern Germany, near the Austrian border, the mountain is known for its scenic beauty and, during the winter, is one of the country's most popular destinations for skiers.

result of alpine, or mountain, glaciation that scoured a variety of jagged features. The highest elevation in Germany is Zugspitze, at 9,721 feet (2,963 meters). The Alpine foreland, or foothills, slopes down to the south bank of the Danube. The city of Munich, (München) with a population of more than one million, is located at the northern end of a pass through the Alps. Precipitation in the Alps can reach 78 inches (198 centimeters) annually, and the rivers of the Alps provide sites for the generation of hydroelectricity.

About 31 percent of Germany is forested. Approximately 45 percent of this forest consists of pine and about 40 percent is beech. Pine is found at higher elevations and on poorer soils. Beech grows in well-drained areas with a temperate climate.

Areas that have been replanted with spruce now make up 20 percent of the productive forest of Germany. Spruce will grow in colder temperatures and are found on the higher elevations of the Alpine region.

Germany supports an abundance of wildlife. Deer are found in the forests, as are martens (large weasels), wildcats, and, in remote areas, wolves. Beaver live along the Elbe River, and wild boars are found in the north. Because of its central location, a wide variety of birds also are found, including those common to both western and eastern Europe. Laws to protect plants and animals have been passed.

ENVIRONMENTAL PROBLEMS

Extensive industrialization has contributed to significant air and water pollution in Germany. The burning of brown lignite coal emits sulfur and other chemicals into the air. These pollutants combine with water vapor in the air to form acid compounds, and when it rains, it is as if vinegar were being poured onto the land. Trees are killed by this acid rain, and when it accumulates in lakes, fish and other animals die. The government has undertaken efforts to control and reduce emissions in western Germany and has closed heavily polluting factories in the former East Germany.

Germany's rivers have been used for the disposal of industrial and municipal wastes and are also polluted by the heavy volume of shipping. Water of the Rhine River is so contaminated that swimming is prohibited. Although the government has now imposed strict regulations, considerable damage has already been done to the aquatic life. The cleanup is very expensive, and it takes a long time to eliminate contaminants from the environment. Large volumes of water are extracted from rivers to be used for cooling, particularly by steel mills, nuclear power plants, and other industries. Water used as a coolant is returned to the rivers at a higher temperature, endangering aquatic life by what is called heat pollution.

The Baltic Sea poses a special environmental problem, because it is almost landlocked. Being nearly enclosed by land, its water is not flushed clean on a regular basis. There are more than a dozen countries that dump pollutants into rivers that flow into the Baltic Sea. Germany has tried to clean up the industrial and municipal waste dumped into the sea by the former East Germany, but it needs the cooperation of other countries if the Baltic is to be rejuvenated. Residue from agricultural chemicals that flow into the Baltic are now the major source of pollution.

Open pit mining, particularly of lignite coal, damages the landscape and releases toxic chemicals into the surface and groundwater. After 1990, about one-third of the mines in East Germany were closed because of environmental concerns. This is a problem of considerable significance also found in the coal mining areas of the United States. Nuclear power plants provide some of Germany's electricity needs. Two plants in East Germany were closed in 1990 due to fears that they were not safe because of maintenance issues.

As was mentioned, one of the serious environmental issues confronting Germans is acid rain, which has devastated forests throughout much of central and northern Europe. Pollution and its causes do not recognize international boundaries. Because winds in the region primarily blow from the west, air masses filled with damaging particles travel eastward from the huge industrial centers of western Europe. Once they reach central Europe, they release acid rain that destroys vegetation. Germany, then, is both a cause and a victim of acid rain and its devastating effects. Faced with this and other critical issues, countries of the European Union are increasingly improving their environmental standards. Thus, Germany is one of the leading supporters for the reduction of greenhouse gasses and industrial pollution, which is enormously significant considering the country is Europe's industrial leader.

Germany is relatively free of devastating environmental hazards. A country's geographic location often contributes to its potential harmony with or threats from the natural environment. The biggest problem in terms of financial damage is flooding. Rivers often spill over onto their surrounding floodplains causing considerable damage. Floods in Germany are mostly the combination of two factors: seasonal snowmelt in the Alps and heavy rains that sometimes occur in the region. They create conditions to which northern Germany's lowlands are particularly vulnerable. Cities are located along the riverbanks, and often spread out barely above the water level, thereby exposing them to rising water. The Rhine, which cuts through a hilly area of western Germany, often floods cities that are located on a narrow floodplain between the river and hill slopes.

3

Germany Through Time

emains of the earliest people known to have lived in the area of present-day Germany were found in the Neander Gorge near the city of Düsseldorf in 1856, thus they were called Neanderthals. They were cave dwellers who lived more than 30,000 years ago. Although a human species, Neanderthals were not entirely identical to present-day humans, *Homo sapiens*. Rather, they represented a distinct branch of humans who prospered in Europe during the Pleistocene (1.6 million to 10,000 years ago), or the "Great Ice Age." For some reason, they disappeared from the stage of history, perhaps because they interbred with more dominant *Homo sapiens* who became contemporary humans. Archaeologists have also found the remains of other Stone Age and Bronze Age people in Germany. The ancestors of the people we now consider Germans came from a variety of tribal groups that developed a common language as a subcategory of the Indo-European family of languages. It is believed that the German language evolved sometime between 1700 B.C. and 300 B.C. in the central and eastern European lowlands.

About 2,000 years ago, Julius Caesar conquered Gaul, present-day France, and led the armies of the Roman Empire east to the Rhine River. The tribes who lived east of the Rhine were able to hold back the Romans, and the Rhine became the border of the Roman Empire. The tribes under Roman control, just west of the Rhine, began to call themselves *Germani*.

Over the next 300 years, tribes east of the Rhine continued to attack the Romans. As the power of Rome declined, the success of these tribes increased. During the fifth century A.D., these tribes were among those who were successful in advancing all the way to the city of Rome itself. In A.D. 476, the last Roman emperor, Romulus Augustulus, surrendered, and the western Roman Empire came to an end.

THE HOLY ROMAN EMPIRE

Following the fall of Rome, for some three centuries, the Franks, who lived in present-day France, grew in power. Although originally a Germanic tribe, they had adopted much of the Romans' cultural system. This is the reason why the French speak a romance language instead of Germanic. In A.D. 771, Charlemagne became king of the Franks. Charlemagne's army expanded the boundaries of his kingdom to include western Germany and northern Italy. When he arrived in Rome in 800, he forced the pope to crown him Charles I, Emperor of the Roman Empire. After Charlemagne's death in 814, his empire began to break up. In the west, the Franks unified to establish the country of France. In the east, the kingdoms of Germany, Burgundy, and Italy were created. The German kingdom included modern Austria and Switzerland. These three kingdoms formed a loose confederation headed by an emperor.

Historians call this territory the Holy Roman Empire, although variations on this title were used during the thousand years it existed. In A.D. 911, the first German king took the title of Roman Emperor.

In the century that followed, Germany developed a feudal system. In this system, people were born into specific classes that determined what they would do. Those with wealth and power became noblemen. They obtained grants of land of various sizes and built castles that were often located on hills for defensive purposes. Many of these castles still dot the German countryside today, where they contribute greatly to the stereotypical image of the country's scenic historical landscapes. The larger landholders could divide their property and give it to lesser nobles. To defend the castles, a class of knights in military service developed. As this system progressed, local power fell into the hands of the nobility, and the king began to lose his powers.

At the bottom of this social system were peasant farmers, called serfs. The serfs lived in small hamlets located on the land below the castle and surrounded by farmland. In return for giving an oath of allegiance to the nobleman and agreeing to fight in his army when needed, the serfs were offered the nobleman's protection. Serfs lived in small huts and often suffered from hunger and illness. Many children died before they became adults, and the average adult only lived to be about 30 years old. In addition to the serfs, there were a few peasants who owned their own land, whereas the less fortunate worked as wage earners. The noblemen were always fighting with each other and with the emperor. The 5 or 6 million people who lived in Germany at this time spoke Old High German, but the only people who could write were the priests and they used Latin.

By 1150, new techniques led to the expansion of agricultural production. Hamlets grew into villages and towns. Some towns grew larger because of their role in the production and trade of various crafts. Craftsmen joined together into guilds that controlled the terms and conditions for the production of particular goods. Businesses needed money, but Christians were not allowed to charge interest on borrowed money, so Jews became the moneylenders. Jews were not allowed to own land, so they had to live in the towns. Often, the Jews lived in one part of the town, and this neighborhood was called the ghetto. As the population of Germany grew to more than 7 million, people started to migrate to the east of the Elbe River. One of the first groups to do this was the Knights of the Teutonic Order, who established the state of Prussia in 1226.

A high stone wall for protection surrounded a typical German town in 1250. Inside the wall and near the center of the town there would be a castle, a church, a guild hall, and a town hall. These buildings represented the major powers of the time: the noblemen, the bishops, the tradesmen, and the wealthy businessmen who usually controlled the local government. The many small political units resulted in a large number of towns, but no single large city. As some towns grew larger, they broke away from the nobles and became independent communities.

In 1273, the Habsburg (also, although incorrectly, known as Hapsburg) family took control of the Holy Roman Empire of the German People, as it was then known. After establishing a set of regulations for the election of future emperors, the Habsburgs were able to hold this position for most of the next 500 years. Primarily through a skillful policy of royal marriages, the family also controlled lands that were outside of the empire, in Spain, Italy, and the Netherlands.

BLACK DEATH AND THE REFORMATION

By 1300, the population of Germany had reached 14 million people, but then tragedy struck. Between 1348 and 1350, the bubonic plague, or Black Death, swept through Europe killing

Der Tanhuser.   lxxviiij.

A German Catholic religious order founded in the twelfth century, the Teutonic Knights played a large role in spreading Christianity to pagan areas of Europe, including Transylvania and the Baltic region. Depicted here on a page from *The Manesse Codex* is Tannhäuser, a German poet and knight of the Teutonic Order.

between 30 and 50 percent of the population. In rural areas, the residents of entire villages died and agricultural production declined, which caused a decrease in the amount of food available. In the cities, Jews were blamed for the plague and many were killed by mobs. Many Jews migrated to eastern Europe to escape this persecution. It is now known that knights returning from the Crusades, in Palestine, probably brought the plague to Europe. Rats traveling as unwanted passengers on their ships served as carriers of the fleas that spread the disease. Plague was a common occurrence in Asia, but was rare in Europe. Once it arrived, however, the impact was comparable to that of smallpox and other European-introduced diseases on American Indians, who had no natural resistance to them. The population quickly recovered, however, and by 1400, it had soared to 16 million.

The development of an educated class outside of the clergy led to the introduction of literature in German, the codification of laws, and the opening of universities. The fifteenth and sixteenth centuries in Europe were the period of the Renaissance, as it was called, in which many such improvements occurred. Although its origins were in Italy, the Renaissance had a profound effect on Germany as well. At this time, the Church taught that people could be saved by performing good deeds, which included making substantial donations to the Church. Thus, the Church grew wealthy. In 1517, German scholar and theologian Martin Luther publicly opposed the idea that people could buy their way into heaven. This was the beginning of the Reformation, the splitting of Christianity into Protestants (the protesters who believed faith was the road to heaven) and Catholics (those who supported the pope's view of good works). Martin Luther was not the earliest critic of the Catholic Church, yet his work led to the most significant changes in western Christianity.

In 1521, Luther translated the Bible into New High German, and with the movable type printing press becoming prevalent in Europe during the previous century, the book spread across the country becoming the standard form for the German language. During the following decade, many of the princes and independent towns, including the duchy of Prussia, converted to Lutheran ideals, in part to gain greater autonomy from papal taxes. Conflicts between Protestants and Catholics developed. In 1555, the Peace of Augsburg allowed the nobility to choose which faith their region would follow. All citizens either had to accept the faith or leave. The independent towns could also choose an official faith; however, many towns did not require their citizens to belong to the chosen faith.

The discovery of the Americas shifted economic power from the Mediterranean realm toward the Atlantic Ocean. As Spain, France, and England grew in importance, overland trade through Germany declined. The economic depression, followed by a series of poor harvests, led to starvation in the rural areas and protests in the towns. This was once again expressed through violence against Jews, who seemed always to be the suspected cause of hard times; hence, the victims of oppression and often violence.

THE THIRTY YEARS' WAR AND THE RISE OF PRUSSIA

The Thirty Years' War was actually a series of conflicts fought between 1618 and 1648 for a variety of reasons. It was a religious war between the Catholic and Protestant states. It was also an internal war between the Holy Roman emperor and the princes of Germany who wanted more independence. In part it was an external war as France and Sweden tried to gain territory and power from the Habsburg Empire. As armies moved back and forth across Germany, it was the farmers who suffered most, as their fields were trampled and armies stole their crops and animals to feed themselves. Sometimes retreating armies burned crops and killed animals so that the advancing army would not have any food. For the farmers it often meant starvation and death. In addition, the armies often brought typhoid and other diseases with them. The population of Germany fell by 30 percent during this time period. Many farmers fled to the cities to seek protection. It took nearly a century to recover from the devastation of the Thirty Years' War.

The Treaty of Westphalia ended the Thirty Years' War. The power of the Habsburg family was reduced in a number of ways. The Spanish Habsburgs had to grant the Netherlands independence, while the Austrian Habsburgs granted Switzerland independence. More than 300 German princes were granted greater sovereignty over their lands; although they remained within the Habsburg-controlled Holy Roman Empire. The treaty stated that the religious affiliations of the states would remain as they were before the war. This gave the Habsburgs, who were Catholic, greater control over Catholic Austria and less control over the Protestant parts of Germany. Perhaps the most significant result of this treaty was its influence on the creation of the nation-state in Europe, and later elsewhere in the world. The concept of nation-state (one nationality of people and the territory they occupy also being a self-governing political territory, or state) remains dominant even in contemporary international relations.

In the years that followed, Prussia wanted to increase its power by developing more farmland. It needed more people to do this. In 1685, Prussia invited about 20,000 Protestants from France, called Huguenots, to settle in its territory. Later, in 1731, Prussia took in 20,000 Protestants from Austria. The Seven Years' War (1756–1763) ended with Prussia gaining territory along the Baltic coast from Poland, and Silesia from Austria.

THE NAPOLEONIC ERA AND INDUSTRIAL REVOLUTION

In 1792, France invaded the Holy Roman Empire and captured all of the land west of the Rhine River. The French legal system was imposed on this area. The feudal system, in which lords had serfs to work the land, was abolished in concert with the experience in the post-1789 Revolution. Two years later, the empire reorganized its remaining territory by joining many of the smaller units to create larger ones.

In 1799, Napoleon became the military dictator of France. The following year, French armies again marched against the empire. Many of the small German states decided it would be best to leave the empire and give their support to Napoleon. In 1806, Napoleon organized these states into the Confederation of the Rhine, marking the end of the Holy Roman Empire.

In 1812, Napoleon was defeated in Russia and the following year in Prussia. His final defeat took place in 1814. The Congress of Vienna met to decide how to reorganize post-Napoleonic Europe. The German Federation was created to replace the Holy Roman Empire. This was a loose federation of 39 states. Prussia gained land in Rhineland and Westphalia and gave up some territory in Poland. This shift to the west brought the German Federation into an area with a larger population and stronger economy.

A long period of peace allowed for population and economic growth in Germany. The conversion of Germany into an industrial nation was the result of a number of factors. First, a growing surplus of farm laborers forced many poor people to migrate into the cities in search of work. Second, the creation of the German Customs Union in 1834 allowed the free movement of trade over a larger area. Third, the steam engine was perfected in the United Kingdom. This new source of power was the basis for new textile factories in the towns, thus providing jobs for migrants. Steamship transportation on the Rhine increased trade and led to the construction of canals. Further, the development of the steam train after 1837 not only improved transportation, but also created a large demand for iron and coal. These were the bases for further

After Otto von Bismarck became prime minister of Prussia in 1862, he set about expanding the German Empire. During the next two decades, Bismarck regained land from Denmark, Austria, and France. Depicted here is the aftermath of the Battle of Königgrätz, which was fought during the Seven Weeks' War in 1866, and effectively brought Austrian control of southern Germany to an end.

industrial growth. The Industrial Revolution led to the growth of cities such as Cologne, Düsseldorf, Essen, Hanover, Leipzig, and Dresden.

THE GERMAN EMPIRE

In 1862, Otto von Bismarck was appointed prime minister of Prussia. He set to work enlarging the boundaries of Prussia through a war with Denmark in 1864, a war with Austria in 1866 that weakened its power over southern Germany, and a war with France in 1870 to regain Alsace and Lorraine. The North German Confederation replaced the German Federation. It converted the member states from a loose confederation into a federal state with the king of Prussia as president and Bismarck as chancellor, or leader of the government. In 1871, Bismarck converted the federation into the German Empire (sometimes referred to as the Second German Empire), with the king of Prussia given a hereditary position as emperor and Bismarck continuing as chancellor.

An economic depression led to renewed persecution of the Jews, and Bismarck also tried to remove Catholics and Socialists from political office. Once the German Empire was created, Bismarck worked hard to maintain peace in Europe by forming alliances with Russia, Austria, and Italy. Conflict between Austria and Russia led to the breakup of the alliance in 1887 and the resignation of Bismarck in 1890.

After Bismarck's departure, the German Empire became more imperialistic. The industrialists wanted access to more raw materials and larger markets for their products. They also wanted an overseas empire like that of Great Britain. The sudden German urge for colonial possession was also politically motivated. Because of late unification, Germany was unable to expand its worldwide influence as did other powers, Great Britain and France in particular. At the end of the nineteenth century, it became obvious that the industrial development of Germany required the type of support other imperial forces enjoyed, thus antagonism between Germany and other countries began to grow. By 1907, Germany's major rivals—France, Great Britain, and Russia—had formed an alliance that threatened Germany. The southeastern corner of Europe, sometimes referred to as the Balkan Peninsula, belonged to the Ottoman Empire, which was centered in modern-day Turkey. By 1912, the power of the Ottoman Empire was declining, and Austria and Russia fought to gain control of this region.

In June 1914, the heir to the Austrian throne, Franz Ferdinand, was assassinated while visiting Sarajevo, in Bosnia and Herzegovina, a former Ottoman Empire province recently annexed by the Habsburg Monarchy. Officials in Vienna accused the Balkan state of Serbia for the assassination and threatened to attack them. Russia agreed to mobilize its army in defense of Serbia. Because of its treaty with Austria, Germany mobilized its army in support of Austria. Germany planned to attack Russia's ally, France, by going through Belgium. Great Britain had guaranteed to support Belgium if it were attacked. Thus all the countries of Europe became engaged in a bitter conflict called World War I, sometimes referred to as the Great War.

In April 1917, the United States entered the war against Germany because German submarines had attacked and sunk U.S. cargo ships in the Atlantic Ocean. On November 9, 1918, the German emperor abdicated his throne and a new republican government was established. On November 11, 1918, the German government surrendered. This event is still remembered each year in the United States as Veterans Day.

THE WEIMAR REPUBLIC AND THE THIRD REICH

The countries involved in World War I signed the Treaty of Versailles on June 28, 1919, to officially end the war. France and Russia were both angry at Germany and wanted revenge. France reclaimed the provinces of Alsace and Lorraine and left occupation troops in that part of Germany west of the Rhine River. On the east side, an enlarged Poland was created by taking the provinces of West Prussia, Upper Silesia, and Posen away from Germany. This separated East Prussia from the rest of Germany. Although Germany only had a few colonies in Africa (Tanzania, Cameroon, Namibia, and Togo) and the Pacific (New Guinea, Carolina, Mariana, Marshall, and the Samoan islands), it had to turn all of these over to the League of Nations, which had only recently been formed in 1920. Finally, a large sum of money had to be paid in reparations.

The government of the newly formed Republic of Germany met in the city of Weimar, thus it was called the Weimar Republic. The German economy was in disarray. Food shortages led to riots in many places and inflation was so high that the currency became worthless. People could not afford to buy food when it was available. The new parliament had so many small parties that no one party could win a majority, or form a lasting alliance with other parties.

After 1924, the situation gradually began to improve. Field Marshall Paul von Hindenburg was chosen as president and treaties were signed to stabilize Germany's borders with France, Belgium, Poland, and Czechoslovakia. The economy began to show signs of vitality after the United States provided loans to cover the reparations and support growth. The government introduced unemployment insurance and improved social housing. Among the middle class, watching movies and listening to the radio became popular pastimes.

The economy was, however, dependent on the United States. When the stock market crash of October 1929 damaged the U.S. economy, it also crushed the German economy. Unemployment tripled in less than a year, and by 1933, almost a third of the workforce was unemployed. The government did not have enough money in the treasury to pay unemployment insurance. People once again were poor and angry.

In 1933, Adolf Hitler, leader of the National Socialist German Workers' Party (the Nazi Party), was elected and appointed chancellor, even though he received only about one-third of the

On January 30, 1933, the National Socialist German Workers' Party
(the Nazi Party) came to power in Germany. Here, Adolf Hitler accepts
President Paul von Hindenburg's offer to become chancellor of Germany
at Garrison Church in Potsdam, Germany.

total vote. Road building and armaments projects created jobs and the economy actually improved during the next five years. The Nazi Party took control of all aspects of society, including unions, agriculture and trade organizations, and youth and women's organizations. The press, radio, and schools were taken over and "un-German" books were burned. Hostility toward "non-Aryans," including Jews, gypsies, and Slavic peoples, began by depriving them of jobs. Conditions grew progressively worse to include property damage and violence. In 1934, the parliament was abolished, and later that year, when Hindenburg died, Hitler combined the posts of president and chancellor and began calling himself Der Führer (the leader). The Third Reich (Empire) was born.

As early as 1925, Hitler had written down his plans for foreign policy in a book called *Mein Kampf.* Shortly after taking power, he began rebuilding the army, navy, and air force in violation of the Treaty of Versailles. When these violations were discovered, Great Britain agreed to allow the German Navy to increase to one-third the size of the British Navy. In 1936, Hitler sent troops into the Rhineland (the disputed region west of the Rhine River), in yet another violation of the treaty. However, France failed to react. The lack of serious response only encouraged the Nazis to become bolder in their attempt to resurrect German greatness (in their own mind-set, of course). Germany and Italy formed the Axis powers and Japan joined in 1938. After putting a pro-Nazi leader in power in Austria, Hitler moved his army into Austria without opposition. Austria became part of Germany, again violating the Treaty of Versailles. Hitler then demanded that the Sudetenland (in neighboring Czechoslovakia) be claimed, because of its sizable ethnic German population. Prime Minister Neville Chamberlain of Great Britain, disillusioned with Hitler's assurances of peace, agreed to allow Germany to occupy parts of Czechoslovakia. This act immediately proved to be one of the greatest political blunders in history and only further encouraged the German leader. In the spring of 1939, Hitler moved troops into the rest of Czechoslovakia, creating a protectorate.

In August 1939, Germany and the Soviet Union signed a pact to divide Poland, but only days later, on September 1, Germany attacked Poland. Great Britain had guaranteed to defend Poland, so three days later, Great Britain and France declared war on Germany. World War II had begun. Germany overran Poland in less than three weeks. Meanwhile, violence toward Jews increased. At first, the plan was to deport them to Africa. Soon, however, they were being lined up and shot. In 1942, three extermination camps were constructed in Poland and a large complex was built in eastern Germany at Auschwitz-Birkenau. This death camp could kill 9,000 people a day. People were killed with poison gas and then their bodies were burned in large ovens. Over the next three years, an estimated 6 million Jews, and countless gypsies, Communists, and other "undesirables" were put to death in these camps in what came to be known as the Holocaust.

In April 1940, Germany occupied Denmark and parts of Norway. In May, Hitler moved quickly through the Netherlands and Belgium and occupied 60 percent of France by mid-June. However, a French free state was set up in the south of France at Vichy. In August, air attacks on Great Britain were begun, but the British Air Force proved superior and no surface attack was attempted. Hungary, Romania, and Bulgaria were persuaded to join the Axis before Germany invaded Yugoslavia and Greece, taking them in less than a month. Finally, in the summer of 1941, Hitler invaded Russia. This was not as easy as the previous campaigns had been and the German troops were not prepared for the long, cold Russian winter. The advance came to a halt. Meanwhile, on December 7, Japan attacked Pearl Harbor and the United States entered the war as a member of the Allies. In support of Japan, Germany declared war on the United States.

After pushing Italian and German troops out of North Africa, the Allies invaded Italy in 1943. The Italian government surrendered and Italy joined the Allies, but German troops continued to fight in Italy until the end of the war. On June 6, 1944 (D-Day), the Allies landed on the French coast at Normandy. The Germans were slowly pushed back toward Germany. On April 30, 1945, Hitler committed suicide, and a week later, on May 8 (V-E, or Victory Day in Europe), the German Army surrendered.

THE DIVISION AND REUNIFICATION OF GERMANY

In 1945, Germany was an occupied country without a government. All of the territory east of the Oder and Neisse rivers was given to Poland. Within the remainder of the country, the Soviet Union occupied the east, whereas France, Great Britain, and the United States occupied the west. In 1949, new constitutions were approved creating the Federal Republic of Germany (West Germany) and the German Democratic Republic (East Germany). Although surrounded by East Germany, the city of Berlin was also divided into eastern and western sections.

With U.S. aid through the Marshall Plan, the West German economy soon recovered. East Germany received aid from the Soviet Union and did not fare as well. Both countries obtained full sovereignty in 1955. Significant migration from east to west led to the closing of the border. Most people migrated by going to West Berlin. East Germany built the Berlin Wall in 1961 to stop people from leaving. The two governments signed a mutual recognition treaty in 1972, and both obtained United Nations membership in 1973. The possibility of reunification seemed unlikely.

Suddenly, in 1989, the Soviet Union loosened its grip on Eastern Europe. Hungary opened its border with Austria and thousands of East Germans used this route to escape. In

November, the East German government removed restrictions on travel. Continuing protests led to the election of a democratic government in the East, and within a year the two countries were unified. The modern-day Federal Republic of Germany was created on October 3, 1990.

4

People
and Culture

Given the devastation of two world wars, it might be expected that the population of Germany would be relatively small. In fact, with slightly more than 82 million people, Germany's population is nearly 20 million larger than that of any other European country except Russia. This chapter examines the people of Germany—their demographic makeup, economic well-being, ethnic and religious groups, the standard of education and health care, and where they live.

DEMOGRAPHICS

The difference between number of births and number of deaths is called the natural increase. In 2007, the birthrate in Germany was 8.22 births per 1,000 people, while the death rate was 10.71/1,000. With more deaths than births, if left only to natural increase, the population would both decrease and grow older over time. Another measure of population growth or decline is the fertility rate. This rate indicates how many children a female will produce during her fertile years, statistically determined to be between 15 and 49 years of age. Since it takes two people to make one child and some children die before they become adults, it is generally argued that if the women in a country have on average 2.1 children, the population will remain stable. If they have more children, it will rise, and if they have fewer it will decline. In Germany, on average, women give birth to 1.34 children. Again, this suggests a decline in population over time. The current rates of natural increase and fertility reflect trends that have existed since the 1970s. These figures result primarily because of lifestyle choices common to residents of wealthy countries. Marriage is postponed and family planning coupled with birth control limits the number of children. The average age of marriage is 26, and only 2 percent of women under age 20 are married. Contraceptives are used by 85 percent of married women between the ages of 15 and 49, and abortion is readily available.

Female employment in the labor force also contributes to a low birthrate. The East German state provided childcare and encouraged women to work outside of the home. In the 1980s, about 83 percent of all women were employed, although few had high-paying jobs. The financial independence of women may have contributed to a high divorce rate.

Female participation in the West German workforce was about 50 percent. Late marriage and the need for two incomes so that a family could obtain material goods were among the main reasons for women working. However, many people believed that a woman's place was in the home and that meant that their jobs tended to be low paying, part time, and not secure. Few women were in top professional jobs. Further, childcare was hard to obtain.

Germany's population characteristics resemble those of most other postindustrial countries. Germans are becoming increasingly concerned over a drastic decline in population. A majority of European nations have experienced a similar problem during recent years. This phenomenon is the exact opposite of those demographic changes that affected nineteenth-century Europe. Then, during rapid industrialization, many factors, including urban growth, improved hygiene and health care, an increased food supply, and need for labor, combined to trigger growth. The Industrial Revolution resulted in rapid population growth first in the United Kingdom and later in Germany and the rest of Europe. The impact was so significant that, despite massive immigration to the New World throughout the nineteenth century, Germany recorded high population growth rates. In the postindustrial era, however, when service industries dominate, the need for a large labor force decreases. At the same time, educational opportunities increase, resulting in improved prosperity that ultimately flows to all socioeconomic strata of the population. With a sharp increase in the number of women pursuing higher education and joining the workforce, marriage is often delayed (or avoided) in order to pursue personal goals. Were it not for high rates of immigration, the United States would be confronted by a similar problem, because America shares similar demographic characteristics.

Another serious issue is the rapidly aging population. Because of low birthrates, almost 20 percent of Germany's population is older than 60 years of age, a number much higher today than several decades ago. If current trends continue, in 50 years, one in every three Germans will be older than 60. Furthermore, the segment of population between 20 and 60 years of age, the workforce, is also aging. That means Germany as a nation is simply becoming older. Such conditions are a burden for any country, no matter how much wealth it possesses. Some cataclysmic projections have Germany's population shrinking so rapidly that the country's population, which currently stands at 82 million, may eventually drop to only 25 million people. More optimistic projections suggest that the population will shrink to only about 70 million, but even that more modest decline will still represent a serious demographic problem.

Despite the decline in the rate of natural population growth, the German population continues to grow in absolute terms. This has occurred because of massive immigration. At the end of World War II, for example, an estimated 12 million people of German ancestry were forced to leave the countries of Eastern Europe and return to Germany. In particular, Germans living in that portion of Germany given to Poland in 1945 moved west. The growth of the West German economy attracted some 2 million migrants from East Germany, most via Berlin, until the construction of the Berlin Wall in 1961.

After 1961, West Germany began to depend on immigration from other areas, particularly Turkey and Yugoslavia, to fill its job vacancies. The removal of the Berlin Wall in 1989 caused a renewed flood of migration to West Germany, estimated at more than 250,000 people per year. Unification of the two countries increased the population of the Federal Republic by 17 million.

ECONOMIC WELL-BEING

About two-thirds of Germany's working population earns its living by what is called the tertiary industries—providing services to others. Only about a third of the workforce is employed in manufacturing. Less than 3 percent work in agriculture, fishing, forestry, or mining, all of which are technologically well developed and hardly resemble the traditional definition of primary industries. The per-capita gross domestic product-purchasing power parity (GDP-PPP) of $31,900 (2007) ranks among the highest in the world. The German fear of inflation as a result of the hyperinflation of 1930 has led to government actions to keep it as low as possible—usually below 2 percent.

The unification of East and West Germany required the raising of taxes to provide social services in East Germany as factories closed and unemployment rose. Unemployment has

Less than 3 percent of Germans work in the agricultural industry; consequently, many seasonal workers from abroad come to Germany to harvest crops. Here, Polish farmworkers sort cucumbers in a field near Freiburg in southern Germany.

been between 10 to 11 percent in recent years, which is more than double the figure for the United States, but not far from the average in western Europe. One reason for such differences in employment rates, even though both Germany and the United States have comparable per-capita GNPs, is because of the welfare state system embedded in the European lifestyle. Germany has a smaller difference between rich and poor people than most other countries in Europe. The highest paid executives earn only six or seven times an average working wage. However, the government relies on value-added tax (sales tax) for much of its revenues and this tends to put a greater burden on those with lower incomes. Typical of citizens of prosperous countries, Germans tend to be materialistic and enjoy having the latest consumer products.

ETHNIC AND RELIGIOUS BACKGROUNDS

German is the first language spoken by more than 91 percent of the population. This means that non-Germans are easily identified. As with English, not all Germans speak the language exactly the same. One of Europe's interesting cultural characteristics is the existence of dialects, which evolved through the centuries. Although they all speak the identical language, residents of southern Germany or Switzerland, for example, can have much different pronunciations than Germans living in the northern states. A similar situation exists in many countries, so it is not unique to Germany. In the English-speaking United Kingdom, for example, more than 50 regional dialects are spoken. Large numbers of German-speaking immigrants from eastern Europe who moved to Germany over the past 40 years also contributed to the variations in the language. The government has tried to encourage use of the "accentless" German of the large cities of central Germany, but in recent years some groups have decided to preserve their local dialects.

Since 1990, there has been a renewed migration from eastern Europe, where ethnic Germans lived for centuries. Many of them resided in the former Soviet Union, or present-day Russia and Kazakhstan. After the Soviet Union dissolved in 1991, many of them relocated to Germany. Ethnic Germans have been living in eastern Europe for several centuries. Many of them were invited to settle in the Russian Empire by the Empress Catherine II, herself of German ancestry. They were skillful farmers who turned the vast Russian steppes into productive agricultural land, but they were also often perceived as being unpatriotic foreigners. Thus, many of them left for the New World at the end of the nineteenth century and settled in North America, especially in the prairies stretching from Kansas, northward through the Dakotas, and even into the Prairie Provinces of Canada. Some, perceived as supporters of the Nazis, were deported to Kazakhstan during World War II. By 1990, more than a million of Kazakhstan's residents were of German ethnic origin. Encouraged by the invitation to "return" to Germany, many decided to come back to the land their ancestors left centuries ago. Those who claim German ancestry obtain automatic citizenship in the Federal Republic, but the government has been trying to limit non-German immigration.

Immigrants from other areas who arrived in Germany beginning in the 1960s were called "guest workers," the implication being that they would at some time return home. At that time Germany, still affected by a loss of workers because of World War II, needed increasing numbers of labor to satisfy demands of the expanding economy. In fact, many immigrants have brought their families to Germany, where they have established permanent homes. Today large numbers of these immigrants have become acculturated (adopting another culture) and their descendants are nearly completely assimilated. Children born of immigrant parents go to German schools, speak German as their primary language, and are entirely integrated into the local lifestyle. This is particularly true of those families in which the parents were rather young when they arrived and who decided to live outside ethnic neighborhoods.

Today in Germany, as elsewhere throughout most of western Europe, integration and ensuing cultural integration (or lack thereof) poses a very serious issue. Germans are concerned with the tendency of immigrants to self-segregate and reject German culture and values. This has been a particularly difficult issue with immigrants from Turkey, who now constitute the largest national minority in the country. Many Turks feel as though they are second-class citizens who have been largely ignored by Germans. Such issues are common within Western countries, because they never had to deal with immigration

More than 3 million Muslims call Germany home, including more than 2 million Turks–the country's largest ethnic group behind Germans. Many Turks live in the Berlin district of Kreuzberg, which is the most densely populated district in the city. Here, a hijab, or Muslim headscarf, is displayed in a shop in Kreuzberg.

problems until recent years. The first generation of immigrants is usually composed of people who work at manual jobs. They are unable to speak the local language and have difficulties climbing the socioeconomic ladder outside of their ethnic neighborhoods. Although it is natural to want to live in areas where they can help their communities and live among their own "kind," sometimes the result is self-segregation and complete lack of socioeconomic interaction with others. Eventually this generates conflict between cultures. Many Germans are uneasy with the issue of the growing immigrant population at a time when native birthrates are at all-time low levels. They do not know how to solve what they perceive to be a huge problem and feel that the future of their country and culture is in danger. The 2005 riots that occurred in neighboring France were the result of similar problems and those events only contributed to the widespread anxiety among Germans.

Today, immigration is the only method of providing enough labor for Germany's economy, and closing the country's borders would lead to serious economic consequences. According to statistical data provided by the German government, some 7.29 million foreigners resided in the country in 2005, a majority of them from Turkey, Italy, Greece, and the former Yugoslavia. Many other ethnicities, however, are also represented in this figure, because immigrants find Germany to be a desirable destination for a better way of life. Not surprisingly, the largest percentage of foreign population lives in the industrial regions and cities of North Rhine-Westphalia, Bavaria, and Baden-Württemberg.

A good indication of the widening scope of immigration is the relative number of "traditional" immigrants versus those from other locations. Immigrants from traditional locations are declining in number, even though the overall number of immigrants continues to increase. This means that these newcomers come from other regions. Indeed, by the end of 2004, some 1.3 million foreign citizens residing in Germany were from non-European (Turkey included) countries. This is an excellent example of how globalization is affecting migration patterns. On the other hand, not all immigrants are from developing countries. The impact of the European Union's free flow of goods and people is noticeable in the change of residency among many western Europeans. Numbers of Dutch, French, Spaniards, and others residing in Germany are measured in hundreds of thousands.

This migration continued even after the economy began to slow down. Between 1990 and 1995, Germany admitted 2.4 million immigrants, including hundreds of thousands of refugees from the war-ravaged former Yugoslavia. As in previous

During the Nazi regime's reign of terror, more than 6 million Jews were killed in Germany. Although the number of German Jews has tripled over the last decade and stands at approximately 100,000, the population is just a fifth of what it was prior to World War II. Pictured here are Jewish rabbis carrying Torah scrolls to their newly constructed synagogue in Munich in November 2006.

times of economic distress, high unemployment has created a situation in which immigrants are no longer as welcome as they once were. A rising antiforeigner sentiment led to attacks on Turkish and African workers, as in 1992, when 17 people were killed in riots. Some of this hostility has expressed itself as a neo-Nazi movement. Economic improvement seems to be the only solution to this problem.

In 1997, the European Union (EU) countries agreed to create an area of "freedom, justice and security," allowing free movement between the 15 member countries, which has now expanded to 27 with the addition of 12 new members. This allowed Italians, Greeks, and Spaniards to move to Germany. Immigrants from Turkey, Albania, and the countries of the former Yugoslavia often enter the EU via Italy or Austria and then move freely into Germany.

The religious affiliation of the population reflects its history and the recent arrivals, including the cultural changes that they introduced. Protestants and Catholics are equally represented with about 34 percent each. As in other western European societies, the impact of secularization has been significant. Furthermore, the legacy of Communism in states of the former East Germany is obvious in regard to religious affiliation, or lack thereof. As an ideology, Communism was opposed to anything but a minute role of religion in society, and this indeed is noticeable in large numbers of people claiming to be atheists, or who simply are not interested in organized religion. Almost a quarter of Germany's people claim no religious affiliation, while many others claim affiliation more as a part of cultural heritage, rather than actually practicing Christianity. Muslims, primarily of Turkish or Yugoslavian background, make up about 3.7 percent of the population. During the Hitler-era pogroms, millions of Jews were put to death and many others fled to what ultimately became Israel, the United States, or elsewhere. Today, only about 100,000 Jews live in Germany. A federal "church tax" pays for the construction of community centers, homes for the elderly, and hospitals, as well as churches.

EDUCATION AND HEALTH

Universal education was provided free of charge in both East and West Germany. It is compulsory from ages 6 to 18. Kindergarten classes begin at age three. Class size is small, with one teacher for every 18 students at the primary level. At age 10, students must make a decision that will have a profound effect on the rest of their life. They must choose between technical schools, which lead to apprenticeships and trade occupations, business schools, which lead to jobs in commerce and the civil service, or academic schools, which lead to university entrance.

Most German children go to public schools, although private schools do exist. Student exchange programs are very popular. Students often travel abroad spending part of the summer in the United States, or the Easter break in the south of France. In addition to school trips, German families also enjoy traveling to other parts of Europe on vacations. Germans often speak several languages, with English being the most popular second language. University entrance is based on success in national tests. There is a definite ranking that identifies the most desirable universities. A large number of adult education centers are also available, and the adult literacy rate is more than 99 percent.

The German higher education system operates somewhat differently than does the American system. In Germany, as is true throughout the rest of Europe, postsecondary education is highly selective and few high school graduates qualify for college admission. The American system, on the other hand, is designed to educate the masses. The trade-off is that, in the United States, educational standards are considerably lower in order to accommodate the many deficiencies that such a system imposes. The problem in European countries, on the other hand, is a rather low percentage of college-educated people when compared to the rest of the population.

Both the German and U.S. systems of higher education have advantages and shortcomings. Moreover, higher education in Germany is funded by the state through a national taxation system; that is, once students qualify through the entrance process, his or her education is nearly free. For several centuries, Germany has been widely respected for its excellent education system. In fact, the growth of many modern fields of academic study, ranging from hard sciences to humanities, took place in nineteenth-century Germany and rapidly diffused elsewhere to become what we know as the contemporary academic world.

German health-care facilities are excellent. The infant mortality rate is a low 4.1 children per 1,000 births, and the maternal mortality rate is 8 women per 100,000 births. The average life expectancy is 79 years. Aging of the population puts stress on the government to provide more health services and social assistance, including old-age pensions. At the same time, the proportion of the population in the workforce contributing tax dollars to pay for those services is declining. This is a problem faced by most developed countries. Municipalities, religious organizations, and private companies provide hospitals. It is estimated that about 43,000 people suffer from HIV/AIDS, and in 2003, fewer than 1,000 deaths were attributed to this disease.

Germany is located at the crossroads of Europe. While this has been important to its growth, it also means that it is a center for international crime, including drug trafficking and terrorism. As with other developed countries, illegal drugs have become a problem in Germany. Heroin comes from southwest Asia, cocaine from Latin America, and synthetic drugs from within Europe. The requirement of the EU to open, rather than to close, Germany's borders makes it difficult for the country to stop this illegal activity.

URBANIZATION

After its political formation, East Germany grew very slowly and still had many small towns and a significant rural population among its 17 million people. In contrast, West Germany grew rapidly and became highly urbanized. In fact, most of West Germany's 62 million people lived in cities. The most densely populated part of Germany is the state of North Rhine-Westphalia with more than 15 million people. Not surprisingly, since the nineteenth century, this state also has

With a population of 3,400,000, Berlin is the seventh-largest city in
Europe and Germany's largest city. Located on the Spree River
in the heart of the North German Plain, Berlin also serves as
Germany's capital.

been the center of Germany's industrial development, a factor
that also contributed to its dense population. One can drive a
car through city after city—from Dortmund to Düsseldorf or
Köln—and barely exit a continuous urban landscape.

As in the United States, people are now beginning to leave
the large cities and live in suburban and rural areas. Excellent road and rail connections allow people to commute long

distances. Some factories are moving out to the rural areas where land costs are lower, wage rates may be lower, and environmental amenities for workers are more desirable. We need to understand, however, that rural areas in western Europe, hence in Germany, are a far cry from what the rural environment used to be. Life in the German countryside is the life of a postindustrial society with excellent living conditions and a highly developed infrastructure. In any corner of the country, it takes only a short drive to reach an *autobahn* (interstate-type highways) and large urban centers. While residents of rural Wyoming or South Dakota, for example, sometimes must drive for several hours just to reach a town with national superstores, rural Germans can hardly imagine such conditions. Although it is a sizable country by European standards, when compared to the United States, Germany is a densely crowded country in which there are few distance gaps. In most of the United States, it is possible to travel several hundred miles by car, even on state and county highways. In Germany, a trip of 100 miles (160 kilometers) in one day on secondary roadways is a major accomplishment!

Berlin, with a city population of 3,400,000 (2005) and a metropolitan population of more than 4 million, is Germany's largest city. The name itself—*Brlin*—is of Slavic origin meaning the area fenced for cattle. Prior to the expansion of Germanic tribes, this area was mainly populated by Slavs. Eventually, they were assimilated into the German culture, and toponyms (place names) were changed to German pronunciation. Frederick the Great of Prussia chose it as the capital of Germany at the end of the eighteenth century. It remained the capital of the German Empire, the Weimar Republic, and Nazi Germany. In 1945, the city, like Germany itself, was divided into east and west, although it was completely surrounded by East Germany. Berlin remained the capital of East Germany, and Bonn was named the "temporary" capital of West Germany. Bonn was a small city on the Rhine and even today has a city population of only 312,295 and a metropolitan population that barely exceeds a half million. In 1990, Berlin again became the capital of the unified German state. However, the upper house of parliament, called the *Bundesrat,* and eight federal ministries remain in Bonn.

The fact that Germany is a collection of many former small states means that there are other large cities throughout the country that first grew as state capitals. Two main axes can be identified. South from the Rhine-Rhur rivers are Cologne (976,000), Essen (585,000), and Düsseldorf (574,000). Along the Main River is Frankfurt (648,000) and the Neckar River, Stuttgart (590,000). Cities east of the Ruhr and just north of the border of the Central Uplands are Hanover (516,000), Leipzig (502,000), and Dresden (500,000). Freestanding cities include Berlin, Hamburg (1.7 million), and Munich (1.3 million). Many of these cities are located on major rivers providing excellent transportation links for their development as industrial centers.

CHAPTER

5

Government and Politics

The modern political history of Germany is usually considered to have begun in 1871, when the German Empire was formed. It will be remembered that prior to this time, Germany consisted of hundreds of very small states that had been gradually unified into the 39 states of the German Federation.

In 1848, representatives were elected to a parliament to discuss German unification. After the formal meetings, representatives with similar opinions began to meet together. These groups became the first political parties. The parliament, however, was disbanded in 1849 without obtaining unification. When the German Empire was established in 1871, an elected parliament was organized. There were a large number of small parties, but they fell into four groups, based on social class. The four groups were conservatives, liberals, Socialists, and Christians. The conservatives were opposed to change and represented the Protestant upper class and the new industrialists. The liberals supported change and came from intellectuals and professionals. The Socialists held most of their support with the working class. The largest party in this group was the Social Democratic Party (SPD). The Catholics were the first religious group to organize to fight anti-Catholic legislation. Their Center Party broadened into a general Christian coalition called the Christian Democratic Union (CDU).

When the Weimar Republic was established at the end of World War I, it also had numerous parties from the four groups listed above, and as a result no party could gain enough seats to have a majority. Indeed, parties would not even cooperate with each other to form a coalition. As a result, there were 20 governments between 1919 and 1933, only four of which lasted a full year. Parties moved toward the extreme right or the extreme left. Growing hostility led to street fighting, assassinations, and property damage that rocked the country. Meanwhile, an obscure labor party known as the National Socialist German Workers' Party (the Nazi Party), led by Adolf Hitler, gained power. By 1930, it was the second-largest party, and in 1933, it formed a minority government. By preventing his opponents from attending the parliament, Hitler was able to pass a law allowing him to make laws without parliamentary approval. After removing all of the existing parties except his own, he passed a law against the formation of new parties, thus creating a one-party state. Hitler also took control of all of the state governments. He called his new government the Third Reich, or empire. It lasted from 1933 until 1945.

At the end of World War II in 1945, Germany was occupied by the Allied forces and divided into four zones. When local and zonal elections were announced, some of the old parties were reorganized and some new parties were formed. In May 1949, the zones occupied by France, Great Britain, and the United States were proclaimed the Federal Republic of Germany and became known as West Germany. Four months later, the area occupied by the Soviet Union was proclaimed the German Democratic Republic and became known as East Germany.

In May 1949, the German zones occupied by France, Great Britain, and the United States after World War II officially became the Federal Republic of Germany, or West Germany. Here, Konrad Adenauer, who served as chancellor of West Germany from 1949 to 1963, leaves the hotel on the Petersberg after officially becoming head of state.

On paper, both countries were quite similar. Like the United States, both would have a national government and state governments, and the head of state in each country would be a president. This form of government is called a federal republic. The federal governments would consist of two houses. The lower chamber, called the *Bundestag*, would be filled by nationally elected representatives. The upper house, the *Bundesrat*, would consist of members appointed by the state governments.

The leader of the government would be elected by the lower house from among its members and would be called the chancellor in West Germany, and the prime minister in East Germany. The president would be elected by the upper house. The constitutions of both countries allowed for their reunification. In reality, the two governments operated quite differently.

WEST GERMANY

The constitution, known as the Basic Law, was adopted in 1949, when the Federal Republic of Germany (West Germany) was created. The Basic Law stated that a party must win at least 5 percent of the total votes cast to have a seat in the parliament. It was hoped that this would eliminate the small splinter parties that destroyed the Weimar Republic. Eleven parties won seats in 1949. The CDU formed a multiparty coalition government. The CDU leader, Konrad Adenauer, was elected chancellor by a single vote; and the Free Democratic Party (FDP) nominee, Theodor Heuss, became the first president. The main opposition party was the SPD.

The CDU remained in power for the next two decades, usually with the support of the FDP. Indeed, for 20 years after 1961 these were the only three parties with seats: the CDU, the SPD, and the much smaller FDP. Adenauer retired in 1963 and his economics minister, Ludwig Erhard, succeeded him as chancellor. During this time, East and West Germany grew further apart.

An economic recession that began in 1965 led to Erhard's resignation as chancellor. In the 1966 elections, the CDU and SPD formed a grand coalition with Kurt-Georg Kiesinger as chancellor. In the next election, the two parties were so close that the FDP could choose the winner. The FDP decided to join with the SPD, putting the CDU into opposition for the first time, although they were still the largest party. SPD leader Willy Brandt became the chancellor. During the 1960s, both the major parties moved toward the political center so there were no strong conflicts pitting right-wing and left-wing interests as had been the case during the Weimar Republic.

The United States and the Soviet Union were now making efforts to get along better and thus America supported Brandt's moves to sign nonaggression treaties with Poland and the Soviet Union. Brandt was awarded the 1971 Nobel Peace Prize. A treaty with East Germany recognizing its existence led to both countries being accepted as members of the United Nations in 1973.

The CDU was able to force an election in 1972, a year before one was due. This plan backfired as both the other parties gained seats. The SPD remained in power until 1982. In 1974, an East German spy was discovered in Brandt's personal staff and Brandt was forced to resign. Helmut Schmidt replaced him. Tensions between Schmidt and the FDP led to the FDP deciding to end its partnership with the SPD and offer its support to the CDU. A new government was formed in 1982 without an election being held. CDU leader Helmut Kohl became chancellor, a position he held through the reunification process and until 1998.

During the late 1970s, a new party began to organize in local and state elections. The Green Party was organized and supported by individuals who rallied around environmental and other important social issues and concerns. For example, they supported recycling with both deposits and refunds on glass and plastics. They also supported public transportation, childcare programs, assistance for the disabled and the elderly, and the peace movement in general. "Greens" were opposed to nuclear power stations. In 1983, the Greens won state elections and subsequently won seats in the Bundestag.

EAST GERMANY

Political parties began to organize in the Soviet-held zone in 1945. The first party to form was the Communist Party of Germany (KPD), but it was followed quickly by the SPD, CDU,

After the end of World War II, Berlin was divided by the United States, Great Britain, and the Soviet Union into sectors within a greater Soviet occupation zone. Pictured here, in 1953, are Soviet troops and tanks in East Berlin attempting to quell a strike by German workers who were protesting restrictive Soviet policies.

and FDP as in the West. In East Germany, the Soviet military kept tight control of the political system. In 1946, the SPD was absorbed into the KPD to form the Socialist Unity Party (SED). When the German Democratic Republic was created, the SED came to power. Unlike other one-party countries, East Germany had opposition parties, but the number of seats they would hold was determined before the elections were held. In theory, the various social groups had representation. The CDU represented churchgoers, the LDP represented the owners of small businesses and professionals, and the Democratic Farmers Party (DBD) represented farmers. The National Democratic

Party (NDPD) was a strong nationalist party with about 40 percent of its membership coming from former Nazi officials. In the 1986 election, the four opposition parties won 52 seats each for a total of 208. The SED and its affiliated organizations representing the working classes won 292 seats.

The leader of the SED, Walter Ulbricht, became the first prime minister. In East Germany, the states were abolished in 1952 and replaced with 15 smaller regions. A one-day strike in 1953 led to Soviet tanks entering the streets. Ulbricht's power became stronger when West Germany demonstrated that it was unwilling to interfere. In 1958, the upper chamber was abolished. When the first president died in 1960, he was replaced with a council of state. A revised constitution in 1968 enshrined the leading role of the SED and limited opposition.

The movement toward friendlier relations with West Germany forced Ulbricht's resignation in 1971 and his replacement by Erich Honecker. In 1972, Western journalists were allowed into East Germany, and the people began to learn more about life outside of their country. The 1974 constitution tried to create an East German national identity and play down the all-German links recently developed.

In 1988, Honecker expressed opposition to the Soviet *perestroika* (reorganization) movement, and a large number of protest groups began to form prior to the May 1989 elections. The SED's proclamation that it had again won the election led to the removal of Honecker and his replacement by Egon Krenz in October. Three weeks later, the government resigned and was replaced by an SED-led coalition. In early December, Gregor Gysi replaced Krenz, and the SED changed its name to the Party of Democratic Socialism (PDS). New elections were announced and 36 parties had registered by February 1990. The first free elections in East Germany were held in March 1990, and the new government opened discussions with West Germany on unification.

The Federal Republic of Germany consists of 16 states, each of which represents a traditional cultural or political region of Germany. In preparation for the celebration marking Germany's fifth anniversary of reunification in 1995, students unfurl a giant flag made up of the 16 individual flags of the German states.

THE CURRENT GOVERNMENT

The current Federal Republic of Germany was proclaimed on October 3, 1990, and National Unity Day was declared a national holiday. Modern Germany consists of 16 states, each representing a traditional cultural or political area in German history. As in the United States, the states vary greatly in area and population. The six former East German states were reestablished, including the city-state of Berlin, and have governments similar to those in the 10 states of West Germany. The Basic Law was extended to all of Germany, and in December 1990, a full national election returned Helmut Kohl as chancellor.

Every citizen who has reached the age of 18 can vote in the Bundestag election and in state and local elections. Elections are held every four years. The constitution allows for any group to run for election as long as their written constitution makes it clear that their aim is not to destroy the democratic system or the republic. Many parties may run for election.

The election process is more complex than that used in the United States. The Bundestag ordinarily has 656 seats, making it the largest freely elected body in the democratic world. Like the United States, Germany is divided into constituencies where party candidates run against each other. Each voter casts a ballot for one candidate, and the person with the largest number of votes is elected. There are 328 constituencies. Much like the larger parties, those parties with strong concentrations of supporters in one area can win seats this way.

In addition to the constituencies, in each state, each elector can cast a second vote for the party of his or her choice. Parties are then given additional seats based on the number of votes they obtained as a proportion of the total votes cast. At least an additional 328 seats are allocated in this way. In addition to the largest parties, this process can give seats to a party with dispersed support, which prevents it from winning a constituency. To prevent the turmoil found during the 1920s, a party must win at least 5 percent of the popular vote to obtain a seat.

In the 1998 elections, five parties won seats. The SPD won 40.9 percent of the popular vote and 298 seats. The CDU placed second with 35.1 percent of the vote and 245 seats. In third place was the Green Party with 6.7 percent of the vote and 47 seats. The other two parties were the FDP with 6.2 percent (43 seats) and the Party for Democratic Socialism (PDS) with 5.1 percent (36 seats). Because the SPD Party did not have a majority of the seats, they formed an alliance with the Green Party to form the government. The leader of the SPD Party, Gerhard Schroeder, was elected chancellor on

October 27, 1998. He obtained 52.7 percent of the votes cast by the members of the Bundestag. Consequently, the FDP lost its role as the ruling party. Surprisingly, the East German SED, renamed the PDS, has won enough votes, all in the former East Germany, to hold seats in the Bundestag since 1990.

The representatives in the upper house, the Bundesrat, are chosen by the 16 state governments. This gives the states far more power than they have in most other federal governments. Each state has between three and six representatives, depending on its population. The representatives of a state must vote as a block. State elections are staggered between federal elections and act as a barometer of national trends. The makeup of the Bundesrat after the 1998 Bundestag elections was as follows: SPD-led states had 26 seats, CDU-led states had 28 seats, and other parties had 15 seats. Regionally popular parties, such as the Republican Party, which won no seats in the Bundestag, may have seats in the Bundesrat. The Green Party is an example of a party that began at the local level, won state elections, and then moved onto the national scene. The Bundesrat has an absolute veto on legislation related to the powers and finances of the states but can be overridden by the Bundestag on other matters. The Bundesrat elects the chief of state, or president, for a four-year term. Johannes Rau was elected president on July 1, 1999. President Rau obtained 57.6 percent of the votes.

The executive branch of the government consists of the president, the chancellor, and a cabinet that is appointed by the president on the recommendation of the chancellor. The SPD and Green Party had cabinet ministers in the government elected in 1998. The total number of cabinet ministers may vary. There are always ministers for foreign policy, finance, defense, internal affairs, justice, and the economy. But areas such as health, education, nutrition, youth and family, labor, and urban and regional development have been joined in various ministries.

The police and court systems in Germany are state run. A Federal Court of Justice is the final court of appeal for civil and criminal cases and a Federal Constitutional Court acts as the final arbitrator with respect to the legality of state and federal legislation. Now, however, the country is subject to laws imposed by the European Union and cannot pass state or federal legislation that would counter such laws.

After years of SPD dominance, the German political landscape was transformed in 2005 with the rebirth of the once-dominant Christian Democratic Union (CDU). In one of the most controversial elections in recent history, the CDU barely edged the SPD, its main competitor. It managed to form a coalition government after a period of political stalemate in which neither side had enough votes to form a solid majority in the parliament. What made this election particularly significant was the appointment of Angela Merkel, a CDU leader, as the new German chancellor. In assuming the office, she broke a long tradition of male dominance in German leadership. This was a rather significant step with a German society that had always favored strong male leaders at all levels of government. It exemplifies the eagerness of Germans to accept changes that were once unimaginable. Perhaps one of the reasons why the CDU won the elections was because of the voters' dissatisfaction with the direction the country's economy was taking. Although the economy is still expanding, it lacks the vigor it once had when it was undeniably the strongest in Europe. Current growth is more gradual, thus Merkel, who is pro-business, is expected to lead the country in the direction of even more successful development. She is also expected to establish a firm German political presence on the international level. Ever since the end of World War II, Germans have felt uncomfortable about interfering in international affairs and their engagement has often been of a limited nature through other bodies, mainly NATO. Now that Germany is not only a powerful nation-state, but also the leader of the European Union, it is becoming clear that the country must reassert itself as a strong economic as well as political leader.

CHAPTER

6

Germany's Economy

Typical of modern industrialized countries, Germany has fewer than 3 percent of its workforce engaged in extractive industries. The North Sea has been a traditional fishing ground with herring being the most important catch. However, over-fishing has resulted in a decline in the fishing industry, and Germany now relies on imported fish to meet its needs. Similarly, the forests of Germany provide about half of the country's wood products. Most of the remainder is imported from Scandinavia.

PRIMARY INDUSTRIES

As described in Chapter 2, agriculture in the north is dominated by the growing of grains and fodder beets to feed cattle, pigs, and sheep. Wheat and corn are grown along the southern edge of the North German Plain, and grapes (for wine) and vegetables are grown in the

Central Uplands. Germany produces significant surpluses of butter, wine, wheat, and meat products.

In the former West Germany, the farms tend to be small with only 5 percent of the land holdings larger than 124 acres (50 hectares). As might be expected with the small plots, nearly half of all operators are part-time farmers. Increased mechanization has resulted in a significant decline in farm labor. In 1949, 20 percent of the workforce was in agriculture, now it is less than 3 percent. In East Germany, cooperative and state farms averaged 11,292 acres (4,570 hectares), but here, too, machinery decreased the number of workers. After 1990, an effort was made to return farmland to its pre-1952 owners. This had the effect of significantly reducing farm size.

Coal and iron mining were the basis for the development of modern industry in Germany. The loss of government subsidies and increasing environmental concerns have led to a reduction in coal production. Coal is being replaced as a source for electricity generation by natural gas, nuclear fuel, and hydroelectricity. Today, much of Germany's iron ore needs are met by imports from France and other countries. Postindustrial economies such as Germany's sometimes find it less expensive to import various products of primary industries from developing nations, rather than investing in their local resources. The main reason is the huge difference in the cost of labor, hence, production versus economic value of agricultural products and minerals. Simply stated, it is less expensive to import the items than to produce them at home. Domestic production also can be discouraged in other ways. For example, the European Union establishes various regulations, such as the need to follow strict environmental guidelines and trade quotas that can limit a country's production. Thus, it often appears easier just to import products from other countries and concentrate more on profit generating service industries.

In recent years, hydroelectricity has become an alternate source of energy for Germans. Here, a worker inspects a turbine at Germany's largest hydroelectric power plant, Jochenstein, which is located on the Danube River near Untergriesbach.

Manufacturing

Germany was one of the first European countries to enter the industrial age. By the 1830s, textiles were being produced in the Rhine uplands in the west, and in the Ore Mountains in the east. The forests of the Central Uplands were cut for charcoal to fuel iron foundries before the development of coal as an energy source. By the 1870s, German industry had moved into the production of chemicals and electrical equipment. Three factors led to rapid growth. First, the government was highly involved in supporting industry. Early interest in free trade to help industries find markets was followed by tariff restrictions on cheap imports after 1878. Secondly, large investment banks had developed to provide the necessary capital, and large firms had formed cartels that could fix the prices of finished products. Companies such as Krupp, Thyssen, and Stinnes date from this period. Finally, although wages were low, the government was the first in Europe to introduce sickness insurance (1883), accident insurance (1884), and old age and disability insurance (1889). Rules regulating working conditions were in place before the turn of the century. Workers were represented by trade unions and the workers' party, the Social Democratic Union, was the largest party in the German Parliament by 1912.

Enormous industrial power supported the armed forces during both world wars. The First World War crippled Germany, but industries were rebuilt in preparation for World War II. The war destroyed much of the transportation system and residential areas, but industry was relatively undamaged. At the end of the war, a large number of skilled people were unemployed and ready to work.

WEST GERMAN GROWTH

The West German economy recovered from World War II rapidly due to a number of factors. In June 1948, a new currency was introduced. Every person was given 40 deutsche marks, providing opportunities for both spending and investment. Stores quickly filled with merchandise.

The United States decided to help rebuild Europe. It hoped to create profitable new markets for American exports and to prevent the expansion of Communism. Between 1947 and 1952, the Marshall Plan provided foreign aid to the countries of Western Europe, including West Germany. West Germany received more that $13 billion in capital goods, as well as management expertise, and this put a highly skilled and relatively cheap labor force back to work. The Organization of European Economic Cooperation (OEEC) administered the Marshall Plan. The OEEC also hoped to reduce tariffs and quotas between member countries to increase trade. Further, the new government of West Germany financed the reconstruction of infrastructure and kept taxes low to encourage business development. Prior to 1955, the government relied on foreign troops for its protection and did not have to spend tax dollars on the military.

West German growth was based on trade, and a number of organizations were developed to increase economic cooperation. In 1950, Germany wanted to import iron ore from France, and France wanted German coal. Trade was improved through the International Ruhr Authority. This evolved into the European Coal and Steel Community (ECSC) with the addition of Belgium, the Netherlands, Luxembourg, and Italy. In 1957, the same six countries formed the European Atomic Energy Commission (Euratom) to develop nuclear power generation. The same year they also organized the European Economic Community (EEC or Common Market) to introduce a series of improvements to be implemented over the next 13 years. These included the removal of internal tariffs and quotas in order to form a free trade area, and the creation of a common set of external tariffs to form a customs union.

Under the EEC, labor would be allowed to move freely between member countries and would have access to the rights and benefits of the host country's welfare system. A Common Agricultural Policy established prices and quotas for many products, a Common Fisheries Policy established national quotas for European waters, and a Common Transportation Policy allowed for the planning of major roads and rail lines. The European Investment Bank provided money for regional infrastructure programs, the European Regional Development Fund provided grants to industry, and the European Social Fund encouraged employment mobility. The 1958 European Monetary Agreement made all currencies exchangeable to the British pound and the French franc, thus encouraging the free movement of capital.

Although West Germany had a free-market system, government policy facilitated economic growth. Low taxes, high interest rates, and low wage increases for workers encouraged investment. The government was also a major employer. Cartels controlled by large companies were allowed to continue in operation. Between 1951 and 1961, the gross national product rose twice as fast as that of the United States, while industrial output rose by 60 percent. Millions of refugees from East Germany and other parts of Eastern Europe created both a market and a labor force. Unemployment was near zero. After the building of the Berlin Wall, hundreds of thousands of Turkish and other foreign workers came to take jobs unfilled or unwanted by upwardly mobile Germans.

The slowing of the economy in 1966 caused a change of government and the introduction of an 11 percent sales tax. The government invested heavily in infrastructure such as expressways, higher education, research, and economic planning. In 1967, the ECSC, Euratom, and the EEC were amalgamated into the European Community (EC).

In 1972, the European Monetary Cooperation Fund stabilized the currencies of the six EC countries within a fixed range. This hurt Germany's trade as the value of the mark increased. In 1978, the currencies were fixed. This allowed businesses to do their bookkeeping in European monetary units, thus eliminating the costs associated with exchange calculations. The European Community was expanded in 1973 with the addition of Great Britain, Ireland, and Denmark. In 1975, the Lome Treaty allowed special trade relationships with 52 former colonies around the world. Greece became the tenth member of the EC in 1981.

The EC is controlled by the Council of Ministers, made up of representatives from each member country. Originally, unanimous consent was required on all policies, but after 1987, a weighted majority vote system was introduced. The policies of the council are implemented by the European Commission, which has the right to create legislation that all member countries must follow. Complaints are taken to the European Court of Justice. All member countries elect members to the European Parliament, where they sit by party and not as country blocks. The Parliament can suggest legislation that should be passed by member countries, but has no overriding authority like that of the European Commission.

Germany supported its farmers by restricting imports and raising the prices of foreign foods to make German products competitive. The Common Agricultural Policy of the European Community deprived the West German farmer of this protection, and many farmers left for better-paying industrial jobs in the cities. There was a drop from 5.2 million to 1.7 million farm laborers between 1950 and 1976, and farm size became larger. This was a migration similar to the one that occurred in the United States at the same time.

Highly dependent on trade and fuel imports, West Germany was hurt by the Organization of Petroleum Exporting Countries (OPEC) oil price increases of 1973 and 1979 and the global recession of the 1970s and 1980s. Increased competition in world export markets from Japan also hurt Germany. Unemployment hovered between 8 and 10 percent, and crisis management tended to replace economic planning. However, the inflation rate remained one of the lowest in Europe. As oil became more expensive, Germany turned to nuclear power to generate electricity and in the 1980s paid for the construction of a natural gas pipeline to Russia to supply fuel despite protests from the United States. In 1985, Spain and Portugal joined the EC and the Single European Act called for a single European market by 1993.

EAST GERMAN GROWTH

East Germany did not follow the same economic path that West Germany did: it had developed a command economy. Collectivization of farmland, machinery, and livestock began in 1952. By the 1960s, the government was encouraging more specialization in fruit, crops, and livestock, and East Germany was nearly self-sufficient in food production even if choices were limited. Small private allotments provided most of the eggs and vegetables.

Based on its prewar industrialization, the government took over factories, or entered into joint ownership agreements. Economic development plans put emphasis on heavy industry, rather than consumer goods. Emphasis also was placed on quantity over quality. In the 1950s, there was a constant labor shortage. Many skilled young men migrated to West Germany, where they provided much-needed labor and helped boost that country's economy. East Germany encouraged women to fill the job openings. Most of the out-migration was through Berlin, so East Germany built the Berlin Wall in 1961 to stop this flow.

In 1963, a new economic system allowed for decentralization and bonus incentives. More emphasis was placed on quality. Fear of political uprisings led to the termination of these programs in 1968. Although more interest was placed in research and technology, East Germany remained a few years behind West Germany in electronics and other consumer goods. The East German economy suffered due to its dependence on oil imports from the Soviet Union. It had to compensate with the use of poor quality lignite coal and the development of nuclear power stations. There were also limited opportunities for foreign trade.

To match the trade arrangements developing in West Germany, the Soviet Union organized a Council for Mutual Economic Assistance (COMECON) that included East Germany and the five other Eastern European states. This was primarily a trade arrangement between the member states and the Soviet Union, although the Eastern European countries were allowed to trade with each other. The main problem was the lack of currency with which to buy goods; thus, much of the interaction involved the exchange or barter of goods. During the 1970s and 1980s, East Germany was the wealthiest of the COMECON countries and had the highest per-capita production in the Eastern bloc. In fact, it rose to the twelfth most important trading nation in the world. Exports included vehicles and machines, chemicals, optical goods, and electronics. About a quarter of all East German trade was with non-COMECON countries. A special trade relationship with West Germany gave it access to the European Economic Community (EEC) as a destination for 8 percent of trade. This provided much-needed access to hard currency. Toll roads to Berlin, compulsory currency exchanges for visitors, and money spent by relatives visiting from the West also added to East Germany's foreign currency holdings.

The removal of barriers to movement between East and West Germany in 1989 created a flood of migrants from the East that numbered in the hundreds of thousands. Neither country's economy could take this demographic change. The West German mark was introduced as the currency of East Germany in the hope that it would lift the economy, but the high-valued mark only caused East Germany to lose exports. This added to the problems of the renewed loss of its labor force. In the West, jobs could not be created fast enough and unemployment rose. This led to attacks on Turkish and other

With the removal of the Berlin Wall in 1989, a flood of immigrants entered West Germany from East Germany. Here, East German border guards shake hands with West German police after removing concrete pieces of the wall to create a passageway between the two sectors of Berlin.

guest workers, many of whom had either brought their families to Germany, or formed families in Germany and did not want to leave.

States of former East Germany still lag economically behind those of West Germany. Even though hundreds of billions of dollars were invested in the former East Germany after the unification, more improvements are necessary. The biggest economic and social obstacle is the high unemployment rate among "easterners" and the lower levels of investment being made in the eastern part of the now unified country. This situation is easily understood; it simply takes time and huge capital investment to completely integrate that part of the country that was split off for almost a half century. The next generation of Germans will, perhaps, enjoy all the benefits of a unified country. For now, however, they continue to face the expensive process of integration.

INDUSTRIAL REGIONS

Unification of the two Germanys was necessary in order to try to stop the flow of migrants by improving conditions in East Germany. Initially, the transition from a command to a capitalist economy led to higher production costs and the closure of unprofitable factories in East Germany. Unemployment became a major problem. The demand for Western goods in East Germany created a small economic recovery in West Germany, but further hurt the East's economy. Food processing and building materials are examples of industries that have declined.

It was hoped that investors from the West would see an opportunity for expansion and profits in the East. The decision of the government to try to return state-owned property to those who had owned it prior to its confiscation some 40 years earlier proved difficult. Consideration of changes that had occurred in the interim posed a particular problem. Western companies had difficulty obtaining clear title to property and therefore preferred to invest in undeveloped sites, rather than taking over existing factories.

Germany is the fourth-largest producer of iron and steel in the world. Production in the Rhur Valley peaked in 1973. As in America's industrial belt, failure to update equipment has resulted in a loss of some world markets; however, Germany still has a reputation for high-quality products. After unification, most of the steel plants in East Germany were closed because they were too inefficient and did not meet environmental laws. The prodution of machinery remains important, particlarly motor vehicles by companies such as Audi, Ford, BMW, Daimler-Benz, Opel, and Volkswagen. The last three firms have opened new plants in the former East Germany. In addition, Bombardier, a Canadian company, has begun manufacturing rail cars in the former East Germany.

Although some oil is extracted on the North German Plain, most of the country's crude oil is imported over 1,560 miles (2,500 kilometers) of pipelines. Lines from Trieste, Genoa, and Marseille bring oil to southern Germany, where it is refined at Karlsruhe and Ingolstadt. Oil is shipped by pipeline, barge, and rail from Rotterdam and is processed in Cologne and Frankfurt. The volume of oil shipments that arrive at Wilhelmshaven make this Germany's third-largest port. This oil is the basis for the chemical industry in the Ruhr. There are also oil refineries in Hamburg. Both Hamburg and Bremen have prospered since unification, as their outlying areas have been increased. New rail and highway connections have been constructed to eastern Germany. Oil piped from Russia is refined at Schwedt on the Oder River and related chemical industries have developed. The chemical industry in Leipzig has declined due to tighter pollution controls. Natural gas is imported from the Netherlands, Norway, and Russia.

Electrical engineering firms such as Siemens, AEG, Telefunken, and Osram are based in Berlin. Germany is also well known for optical and precision instrument companies such as Zeiss. Textiles remain important in the northern Rhine region and southern Germany, but most of the factories in the former East Germany have closed. High-tech industries have developed in the south of Germany in Stuttgart, Munich, and Frankfurt.

THE SERVICE SECTOR

Much like other economically developed countries, most of Germany's workforce is employed in the provision of services. Consumer services include retail and office workers. Business services include law firms, advertising agencies, and accountants. Transportation is an important service industry. Frankfurt is the international air-transport hub for the country and home of Lufthansa Airlines, one of the world's largest state-owned airline companies.

Frankfurt is also the home of the Federal Bank and the stock exchange, making the city the country's financial center. Germany has hundreds of private banks and credit unions providing financial services. The three largest are Deutsche Bank, Dresdner Bank, and Commerzbank.

Government services include public utilities, the post office, telecommunications, and railway, canal, highway, and urban rapid transit services. The main sources of tax revenue are the value-added tax (or sales tax), income tax, petroleum taxes, and corporate taxes. The federal government also collects tobacco and alcohol taxes, and customs duties. The state governments collect motor vehicle taxes and receive equalization payments from the federal government. Local governments collect property taxes and issue trade and entertainment licenses. Germany provides substantial payments to the European Union and pays its share to the United Nations.

One of the particularly significant service industry growth areas is tourism. For decades, Germany has been a popular destination for tourists from throughout the world. Some

Located on the Main River in the western part of Germany, Frankfurt is the country's financial, commercial, and technology center. Here, brokers trade stock at the Frankfurt Stock Exchange, which ranks third in the world with an annual turnover of 5.2 trillion € (deutsche marks) per year.

tourists come to enjoy the country's rich cultural heritage. Others are attracted by quaint villages, clean cities, the majestic Alps with their many ski resorts, or simply to admire the beautiful countryside. Its geographic location contributes significantly to expanding tourism, because it is almost impossible to cross Europe north of the Alps without passing through Germany. Frankfurt is one of the world's busiest airports, and Germany's highway and railroad systems efficiently connect it with other parts of Europe.

THE EUROPEAN UNION

With unification, the former East Germany became a part of the European Community. In 1995, Austria, Sweden, and Finland joined the European Community (EC) and the name was changed to the European Union (EU). In 1992, the Treaty of European Unity (Maastricht Treaty) called for a single currency to be used across all of the member countries by 1999. In 1996, Germany had to cut government spending to stay within the requirements to enter this monetary union. In 1999, 12 of the 15 countries met the requirements for monetary union, and the "euro" was introduced as a common accounting currency. The European Central Bank was based on the German Federal Bank. On January 1, 2002, euro notes and coins were introduced and the national currencies of the 12 countries were phased out. Germany's decision to relinquish use of the mark is a strong indicator of its interest in greater unification within Europe. Although the introduction of the euro was initially welcomed, it also created some undesirable consequences. The shift to a common currency meant that prices had to be transferred from marks to euros in a transparent and reasonable fashion. It soon became obvious that while changing currency, many merchants chose to inflate prices up to 15 or 20 percent and take advantage of customers. During the euro's first months this was a common problem not only in Germany, but throughout most if not all of the EU countries.

The main economic purpose of the EU is to increase internal trade among the member states. Fifty-five percent of Germany's exports go to other EU members, with France (10.2 percent), the United Kingdom (7.9 percent), and Italy (6.9 percent) being the main partners. The United States buys 8.8 percent of all German exports. The major export items include machinery, vehicles, chemicals, metals and manufactured goods, foodstuffs, and textiles. Germany is a trading nation with total exports of $1.133 trillion and total imports of $916.4 billion in 2006. This positive balance of trade creates growth in the economy and allows expenditures for state and locally organized programs.

EU countries account for 52 percent of Germany's imports, with France (8.7 percent), the Netherlands (8.5 percent), and the United Kingdom (6.3 percent) being the main partners. The United States provides 6.6 percent of German imports. Typical of industrialized countries, imports fall into the same categories as exports. German companies also began investing in eastern Europe as soon as those countries entered market economy systems in the aftermath of Communism's downfall. Because of uneven economic strength, eastern European countries were in a position to provide a labor force that was skilled, but demanded much lower salaries than in the West. One of the earliest such ventures, for example, was the purchase of the Czech Republic's automobile company Skoda by German manufacturer Volkswagen. This and other types of investments proved beneficial to both sides. Among eastern European countries, Russia has become, by default, a major partner not only to Germany but also to most of western Europe. Similar to the United States, these countries have a growing demand for fossil fuels from other countries, because domestic production does not meet their demands. Thus, Russia, as one of the world's largest exporters of oil and natural gas, stepped in as western Europe's main supplier. Germany is currently among the leading consumers of Russian gas and both countries are building a pipeline through the Baltic Sea that will connect the two countries directly. The vitality of imported energy to Germany's economy can be most appropriately visualized by noting that consumption of natural gas is five times higher than production, while consumption of oil is about 40 times higher than local production.

7

Living in
Germany Today

Between 1945 and 1990, Germany was divided into a prosperous capitalist West Germany and a poorer Communist East Germany. Nonetheless, people in East Germany lived better than those in other Eastern European countries. Most had a television, a refrigerator, and a car even if they were of poorer quality and came with a high price and a long waiting list. The basics of life, such as food and housing, were cheap and there was no unemployment. Unification brought about both economic and social challenges as East Germans wanted to catch up with West Germany. The federal government tried to help in this process, but there was hostility toward the higher taxes placed on residents of West Germany to improve conditions in East Germany.

In 2006, the United Nations Human Development Index (HDI) ranked Germany as the twenty-first best country in the world in which to live. Germany has an excellent education system leading to apprenticeship programs in 380 different trade, business, technical, and service occupations. A smooth transition from school to work also leads to career advancement within specific occupations and lower levels of underemployment among those who graduated 10 years ago.

Germany grew on a history of worker and business cooperation. This was supported by low business taxes, a low unemployment rate, and an excellent welfare system. In recent years, this situation has changed due to both local and international conditions. Rising unemployment has forced the government to increase taxes and lower benefits. Companies faced with global competition have resorted to decentralization of production by contracting out much of the work, thus reducing the size and power of labor unions.

The change to a postindustrial society means more workers are in white-collar jobs and union membership among white-collar workers is only 20 percent, as compared to 50 percent for blue-collar workers. Young people are not joining unions, as they are more interested in career development. Women, today, make up almost half of the labor force. They tend to work in part-time, nonunion jobs.

Working conditions in Germany are generally good. The German worker has a 40-hour workweek or less, with three to six weeks of paid vacation and numerous public holidays. National holidays include National Unity Day (October 3), Christmas, Easter, and Whitsun, the seventh Sunday after Easter. Corpus Christi and Assumption are celebrated in Catholic areas. There are numerous harvest festivals, wine festivals, beer festivals, and historical celebrations at the local and regional level.

The slowing of economic growth and increase in unemployment has put stress on the welfare system. In 1996, the age of retirement for females was raised to 65, and there was also a significant reduction in sickness pay allowances. Although somewhat reduced, the health and welfare system remains

Festivals are an integral part of German culture and include such celebrations as Oktoberfest (the traditional German fall festival) and Fastnacht (Mardi Gras). Here, children dressed in traditional Bavarian costume prepare for an Oktoberfest parade in Munich.

excellent. A government health insurance program covers about 90 percent of the population and about 90 percent of all health costs. Assistance is based on income and family size. Private insurance is also available and is cheaper for smaller families. Doctors work for both the private and public systems, so there is no difference in health care. The government provides housing for low-income families. When a person has put enough money into a special government savings plan, he or she becomes eligible for government housing loans. Rented accommodations are subject to rent controls to prevent sudden increases. Special programs encourage the redevelopment of inner-city areas.

In 1951, Germany joined the Council of Europe and in 1955, became a full member of the North Atlantic Treaty Organization (NATO). Germany changed its constitution to allow it to have armed forces, and compulsory service was introduced in 1956. Men are required to serve either 18 months in the armed forces or 20 months in other types of service. Germany's army, navy, and air force have become the largest component of NATO in Europe. Germany also has a coast guard and border patrol.

In 2001, the U.S. war on terrorism almost caused the fall of the German government. For the first time since World War II, the government proposed that troops be committed to serve outside of the country. The Green Party strongly opposed this action. As part of the government coalition, there was a fear that the bill might fail and the government collapse. When the vote was taken, the bill passed by just two votes. As a part of NATO forces, German troops have helped attempts to stabilize Afghanistan and, more recently, provided humanitarian assistance in the aftermath of the latest conflict in Lebanon. Ordinary Germans, often reminded by their own turbulent history, lean toward pacifistic means of solving world problems. Antiwar feelings and a strong desire for peaceful dialogue among world nations are widespread.

Germans are known for their love of travel. Half of all adults take at least one vacation a year and many take both winter and summer vacations. Some enjoy skiing in the German, Swiss, or Austrian Alps; others prefer to visit the warm

Mediterranean beaches of France, Italy, or Spain. Germans also love to shop and visit large cities like Paris. Germans make more overseas trips than the citizens of any other country. The opening of borders within the EU has both increased foreign travel by Germans and brought more foreigners into the country.

INFRASTRUCTURE

Germany has an excellent road, rail, air, and water transportation infrastructure. There are 143,898 miles (231,581 kilometers) of paved roads, including about 7,581 miles (12,200 kilometers) of expressway. Even though the Nazis developed the system of fast roads, Germany's famous autobahns, they turned out to be a brilliant transportation idea. Today we could not even imagine Germany, Europe, and many other regions of the world without such superhighways. During the U.S. occupation of Germany, Dwight Eisenhower was so impressed with the efficiency of such roads that upon becoming the American president in 1953, he ordered the creation of our own road network of interstate highways. Traffic congestion is a problem around German cities and the government is trying to encourage rail travel and public transportation. Downtowns often represent a transportation headache, because the centers of old European cities were not designed for automotive transportation, but for horse carriages to pass through narrow, winding streets.

Germany has 29,329 miles (47,201 kilometers) of rail lines. On some lines, trains travel as fast as 155 miles per hour (250 kilometers /hour). In fact, these trains can compete successfully with air travel within the country, because distances between cities are short and it often requires more time to drive to the airport than to reach the railway station. In recent years, the companies ThyssenKrupp and Siemens have been developing a new rail system that would revolutionize ground travel. They

Germany has 143,898 miles (231,581 kilometers) of paved roadway, including 7,581 miles (12,200 kilometers) of expressways. Known as autobahns, the recommended speed on these expressways is 80 miles per hour (130 kilometers per hour). Pictured here is the reconstructed Autobahn 17, which connects Dresden, Germany, with Prague, Czech Republic, and is set to be completed in 2009.

built a train capable of reaching almost 300 miles per hour while levitating on a magnetic monorail. Unfortunately, the first test ride ended in a disastrous accident in September 2006. Germans are, however, determined to continue with its development and implementation.

Navigable natural waterways and canals total 4,640 miles (7,467 kilometers) and allow travel from the North Sea to the Alps and from the Rhine to Berlin. In fact, one can travel by waterway from the mouth of the Rhine in the North Sea all the way to the Black Sea by the main European inland waterway system that connects three rivers: Rhine, Maine, and Danube. This waterway network is economically useful not only to Germany, but to all other countries on these rivers, from Austria to Romania in the east to France and the Netherlands in the west. There are 554 airports, 332 of which have paved runways. Frankfurt (FRA), Germany's main international airport, is one of Europe's three busiest. Road and rail systems in the east have been modernized and integrated with those in the west.

ENTERTAINMENT AND LEISURE TIME

Germany has the most technologically advanced telecommunications system in Europe, using cable, microwave towers, and satellites. There are about 55 million telephones, nearly 51 million Internet users, and some 80 million cellular phones. Germany has both private and public radio stations, including 51 AM radio stations, 787 FM stations, and Deutsche Welle, which broadcasts to the world. There are also 373 private and public television stations in Germany.

Germans also enjoy reading. Every large city has a daily newspaper with special Saturday and Sunday editions, and there are thousands of weekly publications. Laws prohibit any company from trying to gain monopoly control of the media. Most papers do not support any specific political party. There are more than 2,000 publishers producing more than 68,000 book titles a year, which ranks Germany among the world's leading publishing nations, not far from publishing heavyweights such as the United Kingdom and the United States. The annual Frankfurt International Book Fair is the world's leading

Like most European countries, football (soccer) is the most popular sport in Germany. In 2006, Germany hosted the World Cup, but finished third, losing to Italy in the semifinals, 2–0. Here, German fans welcome their team during a 2008 European Cup qualifier match with Ireland in September 2006.

book festival, attracting publishers from more than 110 countries. The largest publisher in Europe is the privately owned Bertelsmann Group.

On weekends, Germans like to attend spectator sports, or take an active part in sporting activities. Soccer and automobile racing are particularly popular. Germans also excel in track and field and in winter sports such as bobsledding and skiing. In fact, German athletes are among the most successful in the world and top performers in the Olympic Games competitions. Soccer, however, is king. The National team has won several world championships, but could only manage a third-place finish in the 2006 World Cup competition that Germany hosted.

Germans often visit friends and relatives and have meals together. Traditional elements of the German diet include meat, potatoes, and cabbage with rye and oat breads. Processed meats are also important, and cities such as Hamburg and Frankfurt got their names from this industry. Beer or wine is consumed with meals. Increased wealth means that today Germans also eat a wide range of "foreign" foods, including many American items. Postindustrial status has brought many positive improvements, such as a wider variety of available foods, in the life of ordinary Germans. Obesity, unfortunately, is not one of them. It is becoming one of the growing social and health-related issues throughout western Europe. The problem of obesity, omnipresent in the United States for many years, is rapidly spreading throughout the postindustrial world. Less-healthy diets and major lifestyle changes that make people increasingly sedentary and physically inactive have made the Germans feel the pressure of the expanding waistline.

Germans attend live entertainment as much as Americans do. Most cities have well-known operas, symphonies, and live theater presentations that include both traditional and contemporary German, as well as foreign, plays. There are many art and film festivals throughout the country. Germany also has more than 2,000 museums and many libraries with historic collections; many are housed in fine examples of buildings from the medieval and baroque periods, which have survived the country's many wars. Many new buildings have also been built. Much of the center of Berlin has been reconstructed over the past decade. A monument to honor Holocaust victims is being built on the site of the former headquarters of the Nazi secret police.

Although Germans face some problems, their way of life today is one of the most comfortable in the world. In the final chapter, we will gaze into a crystal ball and see what the future may hold for the country and its people.

8

Germany Looks Ahead

Charlemagne is often recognized as the founder of the French nation, but he was also responsible for the creation of the Holy Roman Empire and the development of the many small states within the Kingdom of Germany. Somewhat ironically, another French leader, Napoleon, was responsible for the fall of the Holy Roman Empire. From this old empire a new German state would emerge in 1871—the German Empire.

Over the past century, Germany has passed through five stages and is now poised for a prosperous future. In 1900, the German Empire was rapidly industrializing and developing an imperialistic attitude. Having completed an alliance with the Austrian Empire, Germany entered into a war that would involve all of the countries of Europe, as well as many other countries around the world. After the defeat of Germany in 1918, a period of political and economic turmoil existed. This came to an end when Adolf Hitler took control of the government. Hitler moved to reindustrialize and remilitarize the nation. Using the argument of reuniting the German people, he took control of Austria and parts of Czechoslovakia before attacking Poland and starting World War II.

Six years later, Germany was again defeated and the Allied forces occupied all of its territory. Divided into an east and west zone, two Germanys evolved between 1949 and 1989. West Germany again industrialized and joined the military and economic organizations of Western Europe. East Germany was tied to the military and economic organizations of Eastern Europe. The building of the Berlin Wall recognized the barriers between the two countries, but West Germany allowed and encouraged trade and cultural links with East Germany. In 1989, the Berlin Wall came down, and within a year, the two Germanys were reunited. This action was symbolic of the end of the cold war and a greater unity between Western and Eastern Europe in general.

The modern Federal Republic of Germany has the largest population of any state in Europe (excluding Russia) and the continent's strongest economy. As a founding member of the European Economic Community, it is now firmly entrenched in the European Union (EU) and has significant power across the continent. The future of Germany seems bright. The EU continues to bring the countries of western Europe closer together, and Germany, as the strongest member, has the most to gain from this union in the form of increasing markets for its products. Germany and the EU need each other, thus both should grow closer together in the future.

On the global scale, the EU is creating an area with a total population and economic strength equal to that of the United States. There is a clear possibility that the world could evolve from its current condition of having one powerful country, the United States, into a world with another strong country, Germany. However, this division should not be the hostile one evident in the cold war years. The largest ongoing conflict between

A founding member of the European Union, Germany is literally located at the center of the world's largest economic entity. Here, District Chief Erich Pipa (left) and Mayor Juergen Michaelis pose with an EU flag in a field in Gelnhausen, which is near the central German city of Frankfurt and has been calculated to be the geographic center of the European Union.

the United States and the European Union is with respect to subsidies paid to farmers through the Common Agricultural Policy (CAP). This makes American food exports too expensive in Europe. As Germany is a net food importer, the CAP also makes food prices high in Germany; however, it is beneficial to farmers in the former East Germany.

Within Europe there is the ongoing problem of the social and economic integration of eastern Europe and western Europe. While this has moved along in terms of more peaceful relationships, greater economic ties can only take place by offering membership in the European Union. Germany will pay a high price for such a union, because these countries are all weak and heavily dependent on agriculture, while Germany, as the strongest member, makes the largest contribution to the EU budget. The EU has announced that it will not give full membership to any of the countries of eastern Europe before 2010. However, the future integration of eastern Europe into the EU would make the EU the world's dominant trading block.

Germany's economy is dependent upon trade with other nations. Global economic recessions, such as the one associated with the 2001 destruction of New York's World Trade Center by terrorists, decrease German exports, increase unemployment in Germany, and can lead to social unrest. A prosperous Germany in the future is dependent upon a strong global economy.

The unification of East and West Germany showed how the culture of the German people could overcome 40 years of forced separation. Germans are always trying to let people know about their culture. Exchange programs with countries throughout the world are encouraged, and students from the developing countries are encouraged to come to Germany for education and training. The Goethe Institute has branches in 70 countries, which provide information and education about Germany.

Germany has been described as the most stable and ideological moderate democracy in Europe; however, the German people, particularly those in the former East Germany, do not have a strong tradition of democracy. Most of German history has been developed with authoritarian rulers. There is a strong tradition of workers' rights and a strong recognition of social class distinctions. The degree to which government planning directs the economy has not led to public unrest as the considerable powers of the state governments defuse any resentment against the federal government. Continued association with the EU, however, reduces the powers of the state governments and leaves open the possibility of regional unrest and demands for autonomy. At this point in time, it seems unlikely that Germany will split apart as did its neighbor, Czechoslovakia.

Periodic violence against foreigners has raised some concern that there could be a renewed rise of right-wing politics. Currently, both of the major political parties are middle of the road. The extreme right wing is currently divided between three parties, the Republicans, the National Democratic Party, and the German Peoples Party. This has prevented any of them from obtaining the 5 percent of the vote necessary for parliamentary seats. Should it appear likely that they will be successful, the larger parties could shift slightly to the right and prevent any significant growth of the parties of the extreme right wing. The extent to which the German public supports hatred of foreigners is minimal, and should be further reduced as international links increase. Further, the nature of Germany's demographics, which is highlighted by a negative growth rate if the country must solely depend on natural increase, forces the state to encourage immigration if it wants its domestic market to grow. Certainly the Germany of the future will become increasingly multicultural.

The Green Party reflects the degree to which the citizens of Germany have become more conscious of environmental issues than are North Americans. In the former West Germany, action has been taken to improve water quality and encourage recycling. The unification of Germany revealed the large degree to which industrial development in the former East Germany was obtained at the expense of air and water quality. Many factories have been closed because the costs of meeting environmental standards are too high. On the positive side, this has meant that

More than 91 percent of German citizens are ethnic Germans, but due to its decreasing rate of natural increase, Germany will have to allow more immigrants into the country if it hopes to maintain its economic prosperity. Pictured here are two children who represent the future of Germany's demographic makeup.

the development of new industry in the former East Germany has been with modern environmental standards in place.

Domestic tourism is another way for Germany to expand its economy. Germans enjoy spending time outdoors and touring their own country. The coastlines are popular destinations. The

Central Uplands provide a variety of settings for backpacking and outdoor adventure located close to many of the larger cities. Germany's share of the Alps provides settings for skiing and other mountain sports. The major rivers are important for the shipment of goods and also provide scenic vistas, such as the Rhine Gorge, for tour boats. A clean environment also attracts tourists from beyond Germany and further diversifies the economy. Whereas Germany benefits greatly from international tourism, which brings billions of dollars to the country each year, Germans themselves spend even more money traveling within their own country.

At both the national and international level, many of the problems faced as a result of the division of Germany in 1945 have been overcome by its reunification, and the future of the Federal Republic of Germany appears to be filled with promise. It is clearly a leader among European nations and countries of the world.

Physical Geography

Location Central Europe, bordering the Baltic Sea and the North Sea, between the Netherlands and Poland, south of Denmark

Area Total: 137,847 square miles (357,021 square kilometers) [slightly smaller than Montana]; *land:* 216,997 square miles (349,223 square kilometers); *water:* 4,845 square miles (7,798 square kilometers)

Boundaries *Border countries:* Austria, 487 miles (784 kilometers); Belgium, 104 miles (167 kilometers); Czech Republic, 401 miles (646 kilometers); Denmark, 42 miles (68 kilometers); France, 280 miles (451 kilometers); Luxembourg, 86 miles (138 kilometers); Netherlands, 359 miles (577 kilometers); Poland, 283 miles (456 kilometers); Switzerland, 207 miles (334 kilometers)

Climate Temperate and marine; cool, cloudy, wet winters and summers; occasional warm mountain (foehn) wind

Terrain Lowlands in north, uplands in center, Bavarian Alps in south

Elevation Extremes Lowest point is Neuendorf bei Wilster, −11.6 feet (−3.54 meters); highest point is Zugspitze, 9,721 feet (2,963 meters)

Land Use Arable land, 33.13%; permanent crops, 0.6%; other, 66.27% (2005)

Irrigated Land 1,873 square miles (4,850 square kilometers) (2005)

Natural Hazards Flooding

Natural Resources Coal, lignite, natural gas, iron ore, copper, nickel, uranium, potash, salt, construction materials, timber, arable land

Environmental Issues Emissions from coal-burning utilities and industries contribute to air pollution; acid rain, resulting from sulfur dioxide emissions, is damaging forests; pollution in the Baltic Sea from raw sewage and industrial effluents from rivers in eastern Germany; hazardous waste disposal; government established a mechanism for ending the use of nuclear power over the next 15 years; government working to meet EU commitment to identify nature preservation areas in line with the EU's Flora, Fauna, and Habitat directive factory wastes;

deforestation; soil erosion; wildlife populations threatened by illegal hunting

People

Population	82,400,996 (July 2007 est.); males, 40,478,053 (2007 est.); females, 41,922,943 (2007 est.)
Population Density	372 per square mile (231 per square kilometer)
Population Growth Rate	−0.03% (2007 est.)
Net Migration Rate	2.18 migrant(s)/1,000 population (2007 est.)
Fertility Rate	1.4 children born/woman (2007 est.)
Birthrate	8.2 births/1,000 population (2007 est.)
Death Rate	10.71 deaths/1,000 population (2007 est.)
Life Expectancy at Birth	Total population: 79.0 years; male, 76.0 years; female, 82.1 years (2006 est.)
Median Age	43.0 years; male, 41.8 years; female, 44.3 years (2006 est.)
Ethnic Groups	German, 91.5%; Turkish 2.4%; other, 6.1% (made up largely of Greek, Italian, Polish, Russian, Serbo-Croatian, Spanish)
Religion	Protestant, 34%; Roman Catholic, 34%; Muslim, 3.7%; unaffiliated or other, 28.3%
Languages	German (official)
Literacy	(Age 15 and over can read and write) Total population: 99.0% (male, 99.0%; female, 99.0%) (2003 est.)

Economy

Currency	Euro
GDP Purchasing Power Parity (PPP)	$2.63 trillion (2006 est.)
GDP Per Capita	$31,900 (2006 est.)
Labor Force	43.66 million (2006 est.)
Unemployment	7.1% *note:* this is the International Labor Organization's estimated rate for international comparisons; Germany's Federal Employment Office estimated a seasonally adjusted rate of 10.8% (2006 est.)
Labor Force by Occupation	Services, 63.8%; industry, 33.4%; agriculture, 2.8%
Agricultural Products	Potatoes, wheat, barley, sugar beets, fruit, cabbages; cattle, pigs, poultry
Industries	Among the world's largest and most technologically advanced producers of iron, steel, coal, cement,

chemicals, machinery, vehicles, machine tools, electronics, food and beverages, shipbuilding, textiles

Exports $1.133 trillion f.o.b. (2006 est.)

Imports $916.4 billion f.o.b. (2006 est.)

Leading Trade Partners Exports: France, 10.2%; U.S., 8.8%; UK, 7.9%; Italy, 6.9%; Netherlands, 6.1%; Belgium, 5.6%; Austria, 5.4%; Spain, 5.1% (2005). Imports: France, 8.7%; Netherlands, 8.5%; U.S., 6.6%; China, 6.4%; UK, 6.3%; Italy, 5.7%; Belgium, 5.0%; Austria, 4.0%

Export Commodities Machinery, vehicles, chemicals, metals and manufactures, foodstuffs, textiles

Import Commodities Machinery, vehicles, chemicals, foodstuffs, textiles, metals

Transportation Roadways: 143,898 miles (231,581 kilometers), all of which is paved (2003), including 7,581 miles (12,200 kilometers) of expressways; Railways: 29,329 miles (47,201 kilometers); Airports: 554—322 are paved runways (2006); Waterways: 4,640 miles (7,467 kilometers) *note:* Rhine River carries most goods; Main-Danube Canal links North Sea and Black Sea

Government

Country Name Conventional long form: Federal Republic of Germany; Conventional short form: Germany; Local long form: Bundesrepublik Deutschland; Local short form: Deutschland; Former: German Empire, German Republic, German Reich

Capital City Berlin

Type of Government Federal republic

Head of Government Chancellor Angela Merkel (since November 22, 2005)

Independence January 18, 1871 (German Empire unification); divided into four zones of occupation (UK, U.S., USSR, and later, France) in 1945 following World War II; Federal Republic of Germany (FRG or West Germany) proclaimed May 23, 1949 and included the former UK, U.S., and French zones; German Democratic Republic (GDR or East Germany) proclaimed October 7, 1949 and included the former USSR zone; unification of West Germany and East Germany took place

October 3, 1990; all four powers formally relin-
quished rights March 15, 1991

Administrative Divisions 16 states

TV stations	373 (1995)
Radio Stations	838 (AM, 51; FM, 787)
Phones	(Line) 55,046,000; (cell) 79,200,000 million (2005)
Internet Users	50.62 million (2006)

* Source: *CIA-The World Factbook* (2006)

A.D. 800	Charlemagne crowned Roman emperor by pope; controls France, Germany, and northern Italy.
1273	Habsburg family of Austria takes control of Holy Roman Empire.
1517	Martin Luther publicly protests church doctrine on salvation; start of the Reformation.
1648	Treaty of Westphalia ends Thirty Years' War; German princes gain greater autonomy within the Holy Roman Empire.
1806	Napoleon organizes Confederation of the Rhine; end of the Holy Roman Empire.
1871	German Empire formed, controlled by Prussia.
1914	Germany attacks Belgium; World War I begins.
1918	Germany surrenders; emperor abdicates; Weimar Republic formed; signs Versailles Treaty.
1933	Adolf Hitler appointed chancellor; Third Reich created.
1939	Germany attacks Poland; World War II begins.
1945	Germany surrenders; area east of Oder River given to Poland; rest of country occupied.
1949	Federal Republic of Germany (West Germany) and Democratic Republic of Germany (East Germany) created.
1951	European Economic Community formed by Germany, France, Italy, Belgium, the Netherlands, and Luxembourg.
1961	Berlin Wall built to stop migration from East to West Germany.
1967	European Economic Community (EEC) becomes European Community (EC).
1989	Berlin Wall taken down.
1990	Democratic government elected in East Germany in March; unification of East and West Germany on October 3.
1995	Austria, Sweden, and Finland join EC, name changed to European Union (EU).
1998	Federal elections held; Green Party becomes part of government coalition; Germany and 11 other EU members convert to "euro" currency.
2001	Germany participates in war in Afghanistan and two years later in Iraq.
2005	Angela Merkel elected as first German female chancellor.

Glossary

acid rain—Precipitation containing sulfur and other pollutants from industrial smoke that make it acidic.

chancellor—Prime minister, the leader of the government since the time of the German Empire.

Christian Democratic Union (CDU)—One of the two large political parties. It is based on Christian principles and evolved from the Catholic Center Party formed during the German Empire.

Common Agricultural Policy (CAP)—An agreement by the EEC countries guaranteeing a minimum price to farmers on many agricultural products. This raises the price to the consumer.

Council for Mutual Economic Assistance (COMECON)—A trade partnership consisting of East Germany, the Soviet Union, Hungary, Romania, Bulgaria, Czechoslovakia, and Poland.

customs union—An agreement between countries to have common external tariff rates.

East Germany—See GDR

economic union—An agreement between countries to have a wide variety of common economic practices allowing for the free movement of workers and capital between countries.

European Atomic Energy Commission (Euratom)—Consisting of Germany, France, Italy, Belgium, Luxembourg, and the Netherlands to develop the generation of electricity by nuclear power.

European Coal and Steel Community (ECSC)—A free-trade agreement between Germany, France, Italy, Belgium, Luxembourg, and the Netherlands for the movement of coal and steel.

European Community (EC)—Formed in 1967 by the amalgamation of the EEC, Euratom, and ECSC. The United Kingdom, Ireland, and Denmark joined in 1973. Greece joined in 1981 and Spain and Portugal joined in 1985.

European Economic Community (EEC)—A customs union and free-trade area formed in 1957 by Germany, France, Italy, Belgium, Luxembourg, and the Netherlands. Sometimes called the Common Market.

European Union (EU)—An economic union formed in 1995, when Austria, Sweden, and Finland joined the European Community.

federal republic—A country with a president as head of state and a central government that shares or gives control over certain government functions to a number of provincial or state governments.

Federal Republic of Germany (FRG)—A parliamentary democracy formed in 1949 and called West Germany, unified with the GDR in 1990. The term is used for the modern German state.

fertility rate—The average number of children a woman has during her reproductive years (15–49) in a given year.

feudal system—A social and economic system of the Middle Ages in Europe consisting of a small number of wealthy noblemen and a large number of poor tenant farmers.

Free Democratic Party (FDP)—A small political party that evolved from the liberal movement.

free-trade agreement—An agreement between countries to eliminate barriers to trade such as quotas and tariffs.

German Democratic Republic (GDR)—A Soviet-style Communist state formed in 1949 and called East Germany. Unified with the FRG in 1990.

German Empire—The political union of Prussia and 39 other small states in 1871. The empire ended when the emperor abdicated at the end of World War I.

Green Party—A political party that supports environmental responsibility.

Gross National Product (GNP)—The sum of all goods and services produced by a country in a year.

Group of eight (G8)—Most powerful economic countries: United States, Japan, Germany, United Kingdom, France, Italy, Canada, and Russia.

Habsburg Empire—The Habsburg family controlled the Holy Roman Empire as well as territory outside of it including Spain and the Netherlands from 1273 to 1806.

Holy Roman Empire—A loose alliance of states in present-day Germany, Austria, Switzerland, and northern Italy organized after the death of Charlemagne and ending in 1806.

Industrial Revolution—The rise of manufacturing as the main economic activity and the decline in importance of agriculture.

infant mortality rate—The number of children born alive who die before they reach the age of one, per thousand births per year.

natural increase—The number of births minus the number of deaths.

North Atlantic Treaty Organization (NATO)—A military organization consisting of the United States, Canada, and the countries of Western Europe. Organized to defend the members against the spread of Communism and particularly attack by the Soviet Union. Involved in conflict in Yugoslavia.

Organization of Petroleum Exporting Countries (OPEC)—A cartel consisting of the major oil-producing states that attempts to regulate the price of crude oil by controlling supply.

Party for Democratic Socialism (PDS)—The modern SED party with support in the former GDR.

postindustrial society—The decline of manufacturing activities and the rise of service activities as the main economic activity.

Social Democratic Party (SPD)—One of the two large political parties in Germany. It claimed early support from the working class.

Socialist Unity Party (SED)—The Communist-controlled political party in control of the GDR, 1949–1989.

Third Reich—The third empire. Germany under Adolf Hitler from 1933 to 1945.

Warsaw Pact—A military organization consisting of East Germany, the Soviet Union, Hungary, Romania, Bulgaria, Czechoslovakia, and Poland.

Weimar Republic—Created in Weimar in 1918 with the fall of the German Empire. It was a parliamentary democracy in which Adolf Hitler was elected chancellor in 1933. He dissolved the republic.

West Germany—See FRG.

Detwiler, D. S. *A Short History of Germany*. 2nd ed. Carbondale: Southern Illinois University Press, 1989.

Flockton, Chris, ed. *Recasting East Germany: Social Transformation after the GDR*. London: Routledge, 2001.

Fulbrook, Mary. *A Concise History of Germany*. New York: Cambridge University Press, 1990.

Heer, Friedrich. *The Holy Roman Empire*. Translated by Janet Sondheimer. New York: Praeger, 1968.

Jarner, Peter, ed. *Modern Germany: Politics, Society and Culture*. London: Routledge, 1998.

Jones, Alun. *The New Germany: A Human Geography*. New York: Wiley/Longman, 1994.

Katzenstein, P. J. "United Germany in an Integrated Europe." *Current History* 96 (608), 1997: pp. 116–123.

Lang, Thomas, and J. R. Shackleton, eds. *The Political Economy of German Unification*. Providence, R.I.: Beighahn Books, 1998.

Megargee, Geofrey. *Inside Hitler's High Command*. Lawrence: University Press of Kansas, 2000.

Smith, Patricia. *After the Wall: Eastern Germany Since 1989*. Boulder, Colo.: Westview, 1998.

"Who Should Be German Then?" *Economist,* July 4, 1998, p. 45.

Zimmer, Mathias, ed. *Germany: Phoenix in Trouble*. Edmonton: University of Alberta Press, 1997.

Web sites and magazines

Germany's Federal Statistical Office
  http://www.destatis.de/e_home.htm

Radio Deutsche Welle
  http://dw-world.de

The Economist
  www.economist.com

Germany's Embassy in the United States
  http://www.germany.info/relaunch/index.html

CIA Fact Book
  www.odci.gov/cia/publications/factbook/index.html

Further Reading

Biesinger, Joseph A. *Germany: A Reference Guide from the Renaissance to the Present.* New York: Facts on File, 2006.

Flippo, Hyde. *The German Way: Aspects of Behavior, Attitudes, and Customs in the German-Speaking World.* New York: McGraw-Hill, 1996.

Fulbrook, Mary. *A Concise History of Germany.* New York: Cambridge University Press, 2004.

Garner, Simon. *Berlin* (Global Cities). New York: Chelsea House, 2007.

Web sites

European Union Profile of Germany
http://europa.eu/abc/european_countries/eu_members/germany/index_en.htm

BBC News Profile of Germany
http://news.bbc.co.uk/1/hi/world/europe/country_profiles/1047864.stm

U.S. Department of State Profile of Germany
http://www.state.gov/r/pa/ei/bgn/3997.htm

Facts about Germany
http://www.tatsachen-ueber-deutschland.de/index.php?id=1&L=1

Index

Index

About the Contributors

WILLIAM R. HORNE was born in Muskoka, Ontario, Canada. He received his Ph.D. in geography from the University of Lancaster, England. He has taught in England, Canada, West Africa, and the South Pacific, and was nominated for an excellence in teaching award in 2001 and 2002.

ZORAN PAVLOVIĆ is a cultural geographer currently working at Oklahoma State University in Stillwater. *Germany* is the tenth book Pavlović authored, coauthored, or contributed to in the Chelsea House geography book series MODERN WORLD NATIONS. He also authored *Europe* for the MODERN WORLD CULTURES series. In geography, his interests are culture theory, evolution of geographic thought, and geography of viticulture. He was born and raised in southeastern Europe.

CHARLES F. GRITZNER is distinguished professor of geography at South Dakota State University. He is now in his fifth decade of college teaching and research. Much of his career work has focused on geographic education. Gritzner has served as both president and executive director of the National Council for Geographic Education and has received the council's George J. Miller Award for Distinguished Service.